ELECTRONIC SPECTRA

OF

TRANSITION METAL COMPLEXES

Vinod Jena

Assistant Professor
Department of Chemistry
Government College Sarona Kanker CG India

Dr. Manmohan Satnami

Department of Chemistry
Pt Ravishankar Shukla University Raipur CG India

2015

Although great care has not been taken to provide accurate and current information, neither the author nor the publisher, nor anyone else associated with this publication, shall be liable for any loss, damage, or liability directly or indirectly caused or alleged to be caused by this book. The material contained herein is not intended to provide specific advice or recommendations for any specific situation

First Printing: 2015

ISBN-978-1-329-05987-0

DEDICATION

To my friends all over the world.

Thank you all.

Without your support and patience, I would have never achieved my

dream.

ACKNOWLEDGMENTS

I would like to thank my teachers, my editor, my classmates, and my family without whose help this book would never have been completed.

Thank you for your patience and guidance, your use of the editor's red pen...

Introduction to Spectra

Spectra are broadly classified into two groups (i) emission spectra and (ii) absorption spectra.

(i) Emission spectra :-

Emission spectra are of three kinds (a) continuous spectra,(b) band spectra and (c) line spectra.

Continuous spectra: Solids like iron or carbon emit continuous spectra when they are heated until they glow. Continuous spectrum is due to the thermal excitation of the molecules of the substance.

Band spectra: The band spectrum consists of a number of bands of different colours separated by dark regions. The bands are sharply defined at one edge called the head of the band and shade off gradually at the other edge. Band spectrum is emitted by substances in the molecular state when the thermal excitement of the substance is not quite sufficient to break the molecules into continuous atoms.

Line spectra: A line spectrum consists of bright lines in different regions of the visible spectrum against a dark background. All the lines do not have the same intensity. The number of lines, their nature and arrangement depends on the nature of the substance

excited. Line spectra are emitted by vapours of elements. No two elements do ever produce similar line spectra.

ii. Absorption spectra: When a substance is placed between a light source and a spectrometer, the substance absorbs certain part of the spectrum. This spectrum is called the absorption spectrum of the substance.

Electronic absorption spectrum is of two types. d-d spectrum and charge transfer spectrum. d-d spectrum deals with the electronic transitions within the d-orbitals. In the charge - transfer spectrum, electronic transitions occur from metal to ligand or vice-versa.

Electronic spectra of transition metal complexes

Many transition metal complexes are colored. This is due to transitions of electrons between the molecular orbitals that are formed largely by the d orbitals on the metal. Many transitions are in the visible range, with the color of the complex taking on the complementary color of the frequency or frequencies absorbed. Absorption bands in electronic spectra are usually broad, and occur much more rapidly than molecular vibrations. As a result, the spectra represent a "snapshot" of molecules in various vibrational and rotational states. Extinction coefficients will range from <1 up to 50,000 $M^{-1}cm^{-1}$ depending upon the type of electronic transition.

Electronic absorption spectroscopy requires consideration of the following principles:

a. Franck-Condon Principle: Electronic transitions occur in a very short time (about 10-15sec.) and hence the atoms in a molecule do not have time to change position appreciably during electronic transition .So the molecule will find itself with the same molecular configuration and hence the vibrational kinetic energy in the exited state remains the same as it had in the ground state at the moment of absorption.

b. Electronic transitions between vibrational states: Frequently, transitions occur from the ground vibrational level of the ground electronic state to many different vibrational levels of particular excited electronic states. Such transitions may give rise to vibrational fine structure in the main peak of the electronic transition. Since all the molecules are present in the ground vibrational level, nearly all transitions that give rise to a peak in the absorption spectrum will arise from the ground electronic state. If the different excited vibrational levels are represented as $v1, v2$, etc., and the ground state as $v0$, the fine structure in the main peak of the spectrum is assigned to $v0 \rightarrow v0$, $v0 \rightarrow v1$, $v0 \rightarrow v2$, etc., vibrational states. The $v0 \rightarrow v0$ transition is the lowest energy (longest wave length) transition.

c. Symmetry requirement: This requirement is to be satisfied for the transitions discussed above. Electronic transitions occur between split 'd' levels of the central atom giving rise to so called d-d or ligand field spectra. The spectral region where these occur spans the near infrared, visible and U.V. region. Electronic transitions occur between split 'd' levels of the central atom giving rise to so called d-d or ligand field spectra. The spectral region where these occur spans the near infrared, visible and U.V. region.

Ultra-violet(UV)	Visible(Vis)	Near Infrared(INR)
50,000-26,300 cm^{-1}	26,300-12,800 cm^{-1}	12,800 -5000 cm^{-1}
200-380 nm	380-780 nm	780-2000 nm

3. Russel-Saunders or L-S coupling scheme

An orbiting electronic charge produces magnetic field perpendicular to the plane of the orbit. Hence the orbital angular momentum and spin angular momentum have corresponding magnetic vectors. As a result, both of these momenta couple magnetically to give rise to total orbital angular momentum. There are two schemes of coupling: Russel Saunders or L-S coupling and j-j coupling

a. The individual spin angular momenta of the electrons, si each of which has a value of $\pm$ ½, combine to give a resultant spin angular momentum.

$$\sum s_i = S$$

Two spins of each $\pm$ ½ could give a resultant value of S =1 or S= 0; similarly a resultant of three electrons is 1 ½ or ½ . The resultant is expressed in units of $h/2\pi$. The spin multiplicity is given by (2S+1). Hence, If n is the number of unpaired electrons, spin multiplicity is given by n + 1.

b.   The individual orbital angular momenta of electrons, li, each of which may be 0, 1 ,2, 3 , 4 ..... in units of $h/2\pi$ for s, p, d, f, g, ...orbitals respectively, combine to give a resultant orbital angular momentum, L in units of $h/2\pi$. $\sum li = L$

The resultant L may be once again 0, 1, 2, 3,4.... which are referred toas S, P, D, F G,... respectively in units of $h/2\pi$.The orbital multiplicity is given by (2L+1)

0	1	2	3	4	5
S	P	D	F	G	H

c. Now the resultant S and L couple to give a total angular momentum, J. Hence, it is not surprising that J is also quantized in units of $h/2\pi$.The possible values of J quantum number are given as

J= (L+S),(L+S-1),(L+S+2), (L+S-3), ...| L -S |

The symbol | | indicates that the absolute value (L − S) is employed, i.e., no regard is paid to ± sign. Thus for L = 2 and S = 1, the possible J states are 3, 2 and 1 in units of $h/2\pi$.

The individual spin angular momentum, si and the individual orbital angular momentum, li, couple to give total individual angular momentum, ji. This scheme of coupling is known as spin-orbit coupling or j -j coupling.

Term symbols

Term symbols are used to indicate both the electronic configuration and the resultant angular momentum of an atomic state.

The rules governing the term symbol for the ground state according to L-S coupling scheme are given below:

a.   The spin multiplicity is maximized i.e., the electrons occupy degenerate orbitals so as to retain parallel spins as long as possible (Hund's rule).

b.   The orbital angular momentum is also maximized i.e., the orbitals are filled with highest positive m values first.

c. If the sub-shell is less than half-filled, $J = L - S$ and if the sub-shell is more than half -filled, $J = L + S$.

Term symbol of an atom or an ion is represented as

$$^{\text{Spin multiplicity}}L_j = {}^{2S+1}L_j$$

The left-hand superscript of the term is the spin multiplicity, given by 2S+1 and the right- hand subscript is given by J. It should be noted that S is used to represent two things- (a) total spin angular momentum and (b) and total angular momentum when $L = 0$. The above rules are illustrated with examples.

Determine the term symbols

Ti^{3+} $= 3d^1$

$= d^1$

↑				

$S = + \frac{1}{2}$, hence $(2S+1) = 2$

7

$$L=2 \text{ i.e. term is D}$$

and the Ground Term is written as ^2D

$$J=L-S$$
$$2-\tfrac{1}{2}$$
$$=3/2$$
$$\text{Term Symbol}= \quad ^2D_{3/2}$$

V^{3+}

$$= 3d^2$$

$$= d^2$$

↑	↑			

$$S=+1 \text{ hence } (2S+1)=3$$
$$L=2+1$$
$$=3 \text{ i.e. term is F}$$

and the Ground Term is written as ^3F

$$J=L-S$$
$$3-1$$
$$=2$$
$$\text{Term Symbol}= \quad ^3F_2$$

Cr^{3+}

$$= 3d^3$$

$$= d^3$$

↑	↑	↑		

S= + $3/2$ hence (2S+1) = 4
L=2 +1+0
= 3 i.e. term is F
and the Ground Term is written
as ^4F
J=L - S
  =3 -3/2
  = 3/2
Term Symbol = $^4F_{3/2}$

Cr^{2+} $= 3d^4$

                         $= d^4$

↑	↑	↑	↑	

S= + 2 hence (2S+1) = 5
L=2 +1+0-1
= 2 i.e. term is D
and the Ground Term is written
as ^5D
J=L - S
  =2 -2
  = 0
Term Symbol = $^5D_0$

Mn^{2+} $= 3d^5$

Fe^{3+} $= d^5$

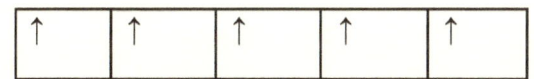

$S = +5/2$ hence $(2S+1) = 6$
$L = 2 + 1 + 0 - 1 - 2$
$= 0$ i.e. term is S
and the Ground Term is written
as ^6S
$J = L + S$
$= 0 + 5/2$
$= 0$
Term Symbol $= {}^6S_{5/2}$

Fe^{2+} $= 3d^6$

        $= d^6$

↑↓	↑	↑	↑	↑

$S = +2$ hence $(2S+1) = 5$
$L = 2 + 1 + 0 - 1 - 2 + 2$
$= 2$ i.e. term is D
and the Ground Term is written
as ^5D
$J = L + S$
$= 2 + 2$
$= 4$
Term Symbol $= {}^5D_4$

Co^{2+} $= 3d^7$

        $= d7^9$

↑↓	↑↓	↑	↑	↑

$S = +3/2$ hence $(2S+1) = 4$

$L = 0+1+2$

$= 3$ i.e. term is F

and the Ground Term is written as ^4F

$J = L + S$

$= 3 + 3/2$

$= 9/2$

Term Symbol $= {}^4F_{9/2}$

Ni^{2+} $= 3d^8$

$= d8$

↑↓	↑↓	↑↓	↑	↑

$S = +1$ hence $(2S+1) = 3$

$L = 2 + 2+1+1+0+0-1-2$

$= 3$ i.e. term is F

and the Ground Term is written as ^3F

$J = L + S$

$= 3 + 1$

$= 4$

Term Symbol $= {}^3F_4$

Cu^{2+} $= 3d^9$

$= d^9$

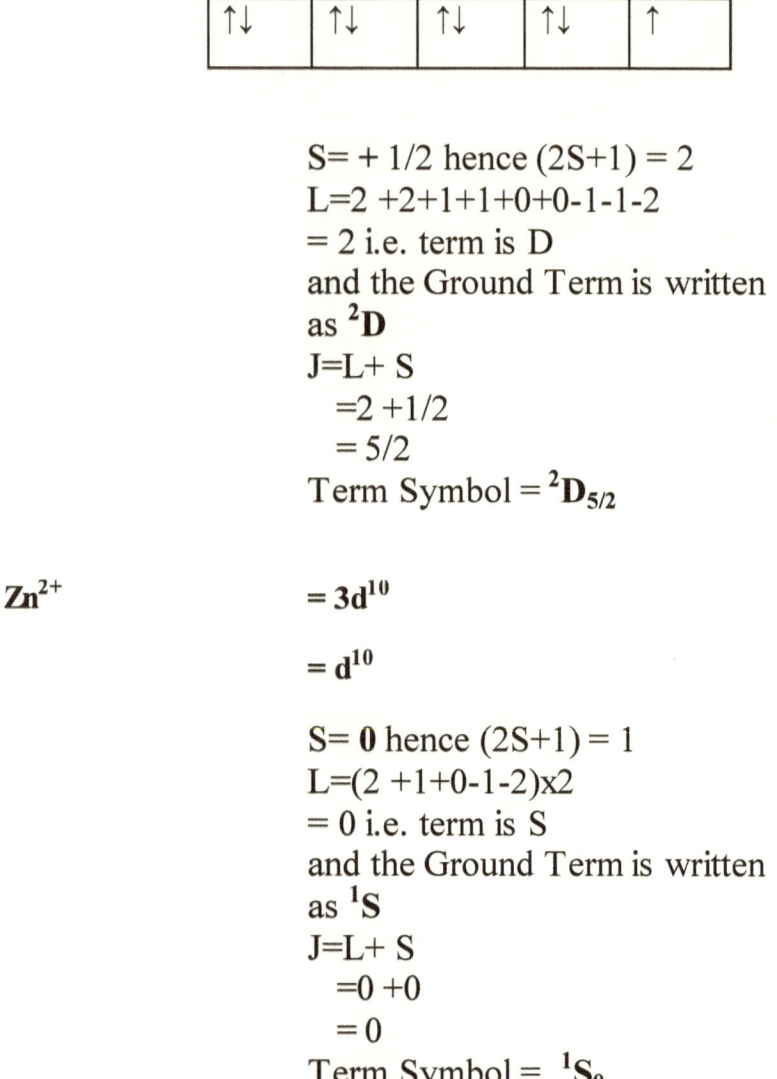

$S = + 1/2$ hence $(2S+1) = 2$
$L = 2 + 2 + 1 + 1 + 0 + 0 - 1 - 1 - 2$
$= 2$ i.e. term is D
and the Ground Term is written
as ^2D
$J = L + S$
$= 2 + 1/2$
$= 5/2$
Term Symbol $= {}^2D_{5/2}$

Zn^{2+}

$= 3d^{10}$

$= d^{10}$

$S = 0$ hence $(2S+1) = 1$
$L = (2 + 1 + 0 - 1 - 2) \times 2$
$= 0$ i.e. term is S
and the Ground Term is written
as ^1S
$J = L + S$
$= 0 + 0$
$= 0$
Term Symbol $= {}^1S_0$

Hunds rule for determination of ground state

1. State with the largest value of S is most stable and stability decreases with decreasing S.

2. For states with same values of S, the state with the largest value of L is the most stable.

3. If states have same values of L and S then, for a subshell that is less than half filled, state with smallest J is most stable; for subshells that are more than half filled, state with largest value of J is most stable

Here we are considering the terms

3D, 3P, 3S, 1D, 1P, 1S. In terms of stability we can rank these terms as 1S ,1P, 1D, 3S,3P, 3D Moststable

Given that the 3D states are most stable,

Simple approach for finding the ground state term symbol for any atom:

1. Find maximum value of S consistent with the Pauli Exclusion Principle $-S= S_{max}$.

2. For $S = S_{max}$, find the maximum value of L consistent with the Pauli Exclusion Principle $-L= L_{max}$.

3. Apply Hund's Rules to find J for most stable state.

- First, arrange the electrons to maximise $S=\sum m_s$.
- (In other words, fill the subshell with spin-up electrons before you add any with spin down.)

- Next, as far as possible consistent with the first rule, arrange the electrons to maximise $L=\sum m\ell$.
- (In other words, fill the orbitals with maximum $m\ell$ first and those with minimum $m\ell$ last.)
- Finally, calculate the total magnetic moment quantum number J according to the following rule:

$$J = \begin{cases} |L - S| & \text{if the subshell is less than half full} \\ |L + S| & \text{if the subshell is more than half full} \end{cases}$$

The first two of these rules are in fact just disguised versions of Coulomb's law. If electrons have the same spin, or if their angular momentum has the same direction, they are less likely to occupy similar regions of space due to the Pauli exclusion principle, and hence their Coulombic repulsion will be lower.

The third of these rules is designed to minimise the energy due to spin-orbit coupling — interaction between the spin and orbital angular momentum terms. However, of the two series of magnetic elements we are considering, this is only applicable to the 4f elements.

For the 4f elements, having calculated S, L, and J in this way, we can calculate the g-factor according to

$$g_J = \frac{3}{2} + \frac{S(S+1) - L(L+1)}{2J(J+1)}$$

and finally an effective magnetic moment according to

$$\mu_{\text{eff}} = g_J \mu_{\text{B}} \sqrt{J(J+1)}.$$

Boron Ground State

Boron, with Z=5 has the 1S and 2S levels filled. They add up to j=0 as do all closed shells. The valence electron is in the 2P state and hence has l =1 ands =1/2. Since the shell is not half full we couple to the lowest

J= | l-s | = 1/2

So the ground state is $^2P_{1/2}$.

m_ℓ	e
1	↑
0	
-1	
$s = \sum m_s = \frac{1}{2}$	
$\ell = \sum m_\ell = 1$	

Carbon Ground State

Carbon, with z =6has the 1S and 2S levels filled giving j =0 as a base. It has two valence 2P electrons. Hund's first rule, maximum total S, tells us to couple the two electron spins to S= 1. This is the symmetric spin state so we'll need to make the space state antisymmetric. Hund's second rule, maximum L, doesn't play a role because only the L =1 state is antisymmetric. The maximum state is symmetric, the next antisymmetric, and the l=0state is again symmetric under interchange. This means l= 1is the only option. Since the shell is not half full we couple to the lowest

$$j = |\ell - s| = 0$$

So the ground state is

$$^3P_0$$

m_ℓ	e
1	↑
0	↑
-1	
$s = \sum m_s = 1$	
$\ell = \sum m_\ell = 1$	

Nitrogen Ground State

Now, with Z= 7 we have three valence 2P electrons and the shell is half full. Hund's first rule , maximum total S, tells us to couple the three electron spins to S =3/2. This is again the symmetric spin state so we'll need to make the space state antisymmetric. We now have the truly nasty problem of figuring out which total L states are totally antisymmetric. Remember, adding two P states together, we get total

$$\ell_{12} = 0, 1, 2$$

.

Adding another P state to each of these gives total l=1 for

$$\ell_{12} = 0 \quad \ell = 0, 1, 2$$

,

$$\ell_{12} = 1$$

for ,

$$\ell = 1, 2, 3$$

and

$$\ell_{12} = 2$$

for .

Hund's second rule, maximum L, doesn't play a role, again, because only the l=0 state is totally antisymmetric. Since the shell is just half full we couple to the

$$j = |\ell - s| = \frac{3}{2}$$

lowest .

So the ground state is

$$^4S_{\frac{3}{2}}$$

.

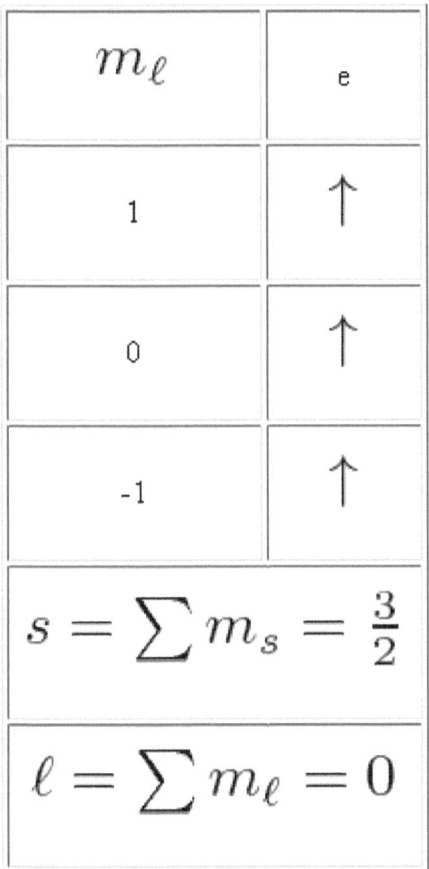

m_ℓ	e
1	↑
0	↑
-1	↑

$$s = \sum m_s = \tfrac{3}{2}$$

$$\ell = \sum m_\ell = 0$$

Oxygen Ground State

Oxygen, with z =8 has the 1S and 2S levels filled giving J= 0 as a base. It has four valence 2P electrons which we will treat as two valence 2P holes. Hund's first rule , maximum total S, tells us to couple the two hole spins to S =1. This is the symmetric spin state so we'll need to make the space state antisymmetric. Hund's second rule, maximum L, doesn't play a role because only the 1 =1 state is antisymmetric. Since the shell is more than half full we couple to the the highest J=l+s =2. So the ground state is

$$^3P_2$$

m_ℓ	e
1	↑↓
0	↑
-1	↑
$s = \sum m_s = 1$	
$\ell = \sum m_\ell = 1$	

Term symbols for excited states

Ne atom

Z=10 i.e $2p^6$

$M_L = m_1 + m_2 + m_3 + m_4 + m_5 + m_6$

$\qquad = 1 = +1 + 0 + 0 + (-1) + (-1) = 0$

$$S = m_{s1} + m_{s2} + m_{s3} + m_{s4} + m_{s5} + m_{s6}$$

$$1/2 \ - \ 1/2 \ + \ 1/2 \ - \ \frac{1}{2} + 1/2 \ -1/2 = 0$$

Thus term is $^1S_0$

Molecular Term Symbols

For diatomic molecules, molecular term symbols can be constructed much like those for atoms. These term symbols label the electronic states of the molecule. For atoms, the term symbols have the form

$$^{2S+1}|M_L|_J$$

For molecules, the term symbols have the form

$$^{2S+1}\Lambda$$

Where Λ is total molecular oribal angular momentum, the parity of the state (g or u) is often listed as a subscript in the molecular term symbol

$$^{2S+1}\Lambda_g \ \text{or} \ ^{2S+1}\Lambda_u$$

where g or u corresponds to either gerade or ungerade parity, respectively. For atoms, the letters S, P, D, and F are used in the term symbol to represent L=0, 1, 2, and 3, respectively. For diatomic molecules, the letters Σ, Π, Δ, and Φ are used in the term symbol to represent $\Lambda=0$, 1, 2, and 3, respectively.

To determine the total molecular orbital angular momentum Λ, start with the electronic configuration. Closed shells such as $\sigma 2$ and $\pi 4$ do not contribute to the term symbol. Only molecular orbitals that are partially filled contribute. Just as each atomic orbital is assigned a particular value of the orbital angular momentum (1) and these values are combined to get the total orbital angular momentum L, a similar procedure is used for molecules. Each molecular orbital is assigned a value of the molecular orbital angular momentum λ. These values are then combined to get the total molecular orbital angular momentum Λ. The table below lists the values of the molecular orbital angular momentum for each type of molecular orbital.

MO type	λ
σ	0
π	± 1
δ	± 2

1.   Molecular Term Symbols for Molecules with Completely Filled Shells For a homonuclear diatomic molecule with completely filled shells and no open shells, such as $\sigma 2$ or $\pi 4$, the electron spins all cancel and therefore the total spin angular momentum is zero,

$S = 0$ (and therefore the multiplicity equals 1, a singlet)

The total molecular orbital angular momentum is also equal to zero, $\Lambda = 0$ (a Σ state)

The parity Ω for a molecular state with all filled shells is always gerade, or g

Therefore, the complete molecular term symbol for the case is

$$^1\Sigma_g$$

2. Molecular Term Symbols for a Single Electron Contributing

For a molecule with one electron in an open shell, such as $\sigma 1$, the total spin angular momentum is the same as the spin of the single electron, $S = s = 1/2$

The total molecular orbital angular momentum is the absolute value of the molecular orbital angular momentum of the single electron,

$$\Lambda = \left| \lambda_1 \right|$$

The parity Ω for the molecular state is the same as the parity of the molecular orbital occupied by the contributing electron.

Example: B_2^+ ion

The electron configuration is $(1\sigma)2(1\sigma^*)2(2\sigma)2(2\sigma^*)2(1\pi)1$.

Only the last part of the configuration, $(1\pi)1$, contributes.

$S = s = \frac{1}{2}$

$M = 2S+1 = 2$ a Doublet

Since the electron is in a π orbital, the molecular orbital angular momentum is $\lambda = \pm 1$

The total molecular orbital angular momentum is therefore

$$\Lambda = |\lambda_1| = 1$$

This corresponds to a Π state and so a term symbol of

$$^2\Pi$$

When parity is included, since the single electron that contributes to the term symbol is in a $1\pi u$ molecular orbital, the parity is ungerade (u). Therefore, the complete molecular term symbol for B_2^+ is

$$^2\Pi_u$$

3. Molecular Term Symbols for Two Electrons Contributing

For a molecule with two electrons contributing in one or more open shells, the total spin angular momentum is determined in the same way as for an atom. That is, the total spin angular momentum takes the values

$$S = |s_1 - s_2|, \ ... \ , |s_1 + s_2|$$

The total molecular orbital angular momentum Λ takes the following values for a molecule with two elecrons contributing,

$$\Lambda = \left| \lambda_1 - \lambda_2 \right|, \quad \left| \lambda_1 + \lambda_2 \right|$$

To determine the parity of the molecular state, the parity of the two molecular orbitals with electrons contributing to the term symbol must be considered. The parities are multiplied together in order to determine the overall parity:

g×g=g, u×u=g, g×u=u, and u×g=u

Example: electron configuration σ1π1

The total spin angular momentum S =

$$S = \left| s_1 - s_2 \right|, \ \dots , \left| s_1 + s_2 \right|$$
$$= \left| \frac{1}{2} - \frac{1}{2} \right|, \ \dots , \left| \frac{1}{2} + \frac{1}{2} \right|$$
$$S = 0, 1.$$

This leads to singlet and triplet multiplicities, $2S+1 = 1$ or 3

The molecular orbital angular momentum for the electron in the σ orbital is $\lambda 1 = 0$ and the molecular orbital angular momentum for the electron in the π orbital is $\lambda 2 = \pm 1$

The total molecular orbital angular momentum is therefore

$$\Lambda = \left| 0 - (-1) \right|, \quad \left| 0 + (-1) \right|$$

when considering the combination of $\lambda 1 = 0$ and $\lambda 2 = -1$, and

$$\Lambda = \left|0 - 1\right| , \left|0 + 1\right|$$

when considering the combination of of $\lambda 1 = 0$ and $\lambda 2 = 1$,

All of these combinations lead to the value

$$\Lambda = 1 ;$$

This is a Π state. The term symbols possible for this electron configuration are therefore

$$^1\Pi \text{ and } {}^3\Pi$$

Term Symbol	Atoms $^{2S+1}L_J$	Molecules $^{2S+1}[M_L]_{g/u}$
Orbital Momentum -along z-axis	Choices of z-axis is arbitrary for spherical atom m_l= component along z-axis for individual electron M_L= →$\sum ml,i$	z-axis defined as internuclear axis, P_o m_l= component along z-axis for individual electron M_L= →$\sum ml,i$ $\|M_L\| = 1:\sum$ (s=sigma) = 2: Л (p=pi) = 3; Δ (d=delta)
-Total	L=1:P, 2:D, 3:F	L not fully applicable for molecules due to lower symmetry of molecules(not spheres)
Electron Spin -along z-axis Total	ms= ±1/2 M_s= →$\sum m s,i$ Spin multiplicity = 2S+1	ms= ±1/2 M_s= →$\sum m s,i$ Spin multiplicity = 2S+1
Total combined Angular momentum	J= L+S = L+S, L+S-1,.........|L-S|	
Inversion Symmetry		If inversion symmetry exits; gi*gu = g ui*uj = g gi*uj =u

Example 1: H_2

MO Configuration: $1\sigma_g^2$

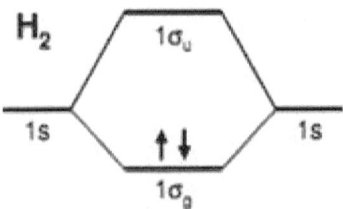

Spin: All electrons are paired therefore

$$Ms = 0$$

so that $S = 0$ and $M_l = 0$

$1\sigma_g \ (m_l{=}0)$	↑↓
$M_S = \Sigma m_s$	0

Inversion symmetry g/u

H_2 has inversion symmetry , thus g/u notation is applicable and as electron 1 is in gMO and 2 in gMO so that

g1 *g2 = g

Term Symbol $=^1\Sigma_g$

Example 2: H_2^-

MO Configuration $= 1\sigma_g^2 1\sigma_u^2$

$1\sigma_g^2$ is fully occupied and $1\sigma_u^1$ is partially occupied with a single electron

$1\sigma_g$		
$1\sigma_u$ $(m_l = 0)$	↑	↓
M_S	½	-½

Spin $= 2s+1 = 2*1/2 + 1 = 2$

Angular Momentum:

Electron is in a σ orbital made up of is so ms $=0$ for that electron

Therefore $|M_L| = 0 \; (\Sigma)$

Inversion symmetry g/u

H_2^- has inversion symmetry , thus g/u notation is applicable

The one elctron is an unfilled suborbital is in a u orbital, therefore total g/u symmetry is u

Term Symbol $= {}^2\Sigma_g$

SELECTION RULES FOR ELECTRONIC TRANSITIONS

Selection rules

The Selection Rules governing transitions between electronic energy levels of transition metal complexes are:

1. $\Delta S = 0$ The Spin Rule
2. $\Delta l = +/- 1$ The Orbital Rule (Laporte)

The first rule says that allowed transitions must involve the promotion of electrons without a change in their spin.

The second rule says that if the molecule has a centre of symmetry, transitions within a given set of p or d orbitals (i.e. those which only involve a redistribution of electrons within a given subshell) are forbidden.

Relaxation of the Rules can occur through:

a) Spin-Orbit coupling - this gives rise to weak spin forbidden bands

b) Vibronic coupling - an octahedral complex may have allowed vibrations where the molecule is asymmetric. Absorption of light at that moment is then possible.

31

c) π-acceptor and π-donor ligands can mix with the d-orbitals so transitions are no longer purely d-d.

Types of transition

1. Charge transfer, either ligand to metal or metal to ligand. These are often extremely intense and are generally found in the UV but they may have a tail into the visible.

2. d-d, these can occur in both the UV and visible region but since they are forbidden transitions have small intensities.

Expected Intensities of Electronic transitions

Transition	Example	Typical Values $\epsilon/m^2 mol^{-1}$
Spin forbidden Laporte forbidden	$[Mn(H_2O)_6]^{2+}$	0.1
Spin allowed (Oh complex) Laporte forbidden	$[Ti(H_2O)_6]^{3+}$	1 - 10
Spin allowed (T_d complex) Laporte partially allowed by d-p mixing	$[CoCl_4]^{2-}$	50 - 150
Spin allowed Laporte allowed Ex charge transfer bands	$[TiCl_6]^{2-}$ or MnO_4^-	$1000 - 10^6$

LaPorte selection rule

This rule says that transitions between the orbitals of the same sub shell are forbidden. In other words, the for total orbital angular momentum is $\Delta L = \pm 1$. This is La Porte allowed transitions. Thus transition such as $1S \rightarrow 1P$ and $2D \rightarrow 2P$ are allowed but transition such as $3D \rightarrow 3S$ is forbidden since $\Delta L = -2$ .That is, transition should involve a change of one unit of angular momentum. Hence transitions from gerade to ungerade (g to u) or vice versa are allowed, i.e., $u \rightarrow$ g or g $\rightarrow$ ubut not u $\rightarrow$ uorg $\rightarrow$ g. In the case of p sub shell, both ground and excited states are odd and in the case of d sub shell both ground and excited states are even. As a rule transition should be from even to odd or vice versa.

The same rule is also stated in the form of a statement instead of an equation:

Electronic transitions within the same p or d sub-shell are forbidden, if the molecule has centre of symmetry.

Spin selection rule

There can be no change in the multiplicity (or total spin) during a transition, $\Delta S = 0$. Therefore, singlet states must be excited to other singlet states, triplet states must be excited to other triplet states, etc. No transitions from singlet to triplet or other situations where the multiplicity changes are allowed.

Thus transitions such as $^2S \rightarrow ^2P$ and $^3D \rightarrow ^3P$ are allowed, but transition such as $^1S \rightarrow ^3P$ is forbidden. The same rule is also stated in the form of a statement, Electronic Transitions between the different states of spin multiplicity are forbidden.

The selection Rule for total angular momentum, J, is

$\Delta J = 0$ or ± 1

The transitions such as $^2P_{1/2} \rightarrow ^2D_{3/2}$ and $^2P_{3/2} \rightarrow ^2D_{3/2}$ are allowed, but transition such as $^2P_{1/2} \rightarrow ^2D_{5/2}$ is forbidden since $\Delta J = 2$. There is no selection rule governing the change in the value of n, the principal quantum number. Thus in hydrogen, transitions such as $1s \rightarrow 2p$, $1s \rightarrow 3p$, $1s \rightarrow 4p$ are allowed.

Usually, electronic absorption is indicated by reverse arrow, $\leftarrow$, and emission is indicated by the forward arrow, $\rightarrow$, though this rule is not strictly obeyed

Mechanism of breakdown of selection rules

Spin-orbit coupling

For electronic transition to take place, $\Delta S = 0$ and $\Delta L = \pm 1$ in the absence of spin-orbit coupling. However, spin and orbital motions are coupled. Even, if they are coupled very weakly, a little of each spin state mixes with the other in the ground and excited states by an amount dependent upon the energy difference in the orbital states and magnitude of spin –orbit coupling constant.

Therefore electronic transitions occur between different states of spin multiplicity and also between states in which ΔL is not equal to ± 1. For example, if the ground state were 99% singlet and 1% triplet (due to spin– orbit coupling) and the excited state were 1% singlet and 99 % triplet, then the intensity would derive from the triplet –triplet and singlet-singlet interactions. Spin-orbit coupling provides small energy differences between degenerate states.

This coupling is of two types. The single electron spin orbit coupling parameter ζ, gives the strength of the interaction between the spin and orbital angular momenta of a single electron for a particular configuration. The other parameter, λ, is the property of the term.

For high spin complexes,

$$\lambda = \pm \, \xi/2S$$

Here positive sign holds for shells less than half field and negative sign holds for more than half filled shells. S is the same as the one given for the free ion. The λ values in crystals are close to their free ion values. Λ decreases in crystal with decreasing Racah parameters B and C. For high spin d5configuration, there is no spin orbit coupling because 6S state is unaffected by the ligand fields. The λ and ζ values for 3d series are given in Table.

Ion	Ti(II)	V(II)	Cr(II)	Mn(II)	Fe(II)	Co(II)	Ni(II)
ζ (cm^{-1})	121	167	230	347	410	533	649
λ (cm^{-1})	60	56	57	0	-102	-177	-325

La Porte selection rule

Physically 3d (even) and 4p (odd) wave functions may be mixed, if centre of inversion (i) is removed. There are two processes by which i is removed.

   a. The central metal ion is placed in a distorted field (tetrahedral field, Tetragonal distortions, etc.,) The most important case of distorted or asymmetric field is the case of a tetrahedral complex. Tetrahedron has no inversion centre and so d-p mixing takes place. So electronic transitions in tetrahedral complexes are much more intense, often by a factor 100, than in a analogous octahedral complexes.

Transisomer of $[Co(en)_2Cl_2]$ +in aqueous solution is three to four times less intense than the cisisomer because the former is centro-symmetric. Other types of distortion include Jahn –Teller distortions.

b. Odd vibrations of the surrounding ligands create the distorted field for a time that is long enough compared to the time necessary for the electronic transition to occur (Franck Condon Principle).Certain vibrations will remove the centre of symmetry. Mathematically this implies coupling of vibrational and electronic wave functions. Breaking down of La Porte rule by vibrionic coupling has been termed as "Intensity Stealing". If the forbiddenexcited term lies energetically nearby a fully allowed transition, it would produce a very intense band. Intensity Stealing by this mechanism decreases in magnitude with increasing energy separation between the excited term and the allowed level.

Total Molecular Orbital Angular Momentum Selection Rule

The selection rule involving the total molecular orbital angular momentum is

$$\Delta\Lambda = 0, \pm 1$$

Thus, transitions such as

$$\Sigma \rightarrow \Sigma, \Pi \rightarrow \Pi, \Delta \rightarrow \Delta,$$

etc. are allowed because they all correspond to

$$\Delta\Lambda = 0$$

In addition, transitions such as

$$\Sigma \rightarrow \Pi \text{ or } \Pi \rightarrow \Sigma, \Pi \rightarrow \Delta \text{ or } \Delta \rightarrow \Pi, \Delta \rightarrow \Phi \text{ or } \Phi \rightarrow \Delta$$

etc., also are allowed because they correspond to

$$\Delta\Lambda = +1 \ \left(\text{or } -1 \right)$$

Parity Selection Rule

In order for a transition to be allowed, the parity must change during the transition. That is, transitions must involve a parity change of either g $\rightarrow$ g or u$\rightarrow$g. Transitions from g$\rightarrow$g and u $\rightarrow$u are not allowed

The Crystal Field Splitting of Russell-Saunders terms

When a metal ion is surrounded by ligands in a coordination compound, those ligands generate an electrostatic field that removes the degeneracy of the d orbitals. The result is that e g and t_{2g} subsets of orbitals are produced. Because the d orbitals are no longer degenerate, spin-orbit coupling is altered. However, just as the d orbitals are split in terms of their energies, the spectroscopic states are split in the ligand field. The spectroscopic states are split into components that have the same multiplicity as the free ion states from which they arise. A single electron in a d orbital gives rise to a ^2D term for the gaseous ion, but in an octahedral field the electron will reside in a t_{2g} orbital, and the spectroscopic state for the t_{2g}^1 configuration is $^2T_{2g}$. If the electron were excited to an e_g orbital, the spectroscopic state would be ^2E_g. Thus, transitions between $^2T_{2g}$ and ^2E_g states would not be spin forbidden because both states are doublets

The magnitude of the d orbital splitting is generally represented as a fraction of Δ_{oct} or 10Dq. The ground term energies for free ions are also affected by the influence of a crystal field and an analogy is made between orbitals and ground terms that are related due to the angular parts of their electron distribution. The effect of a crystal field on different orbitals in an octahedral field environment will cause the d orbitals to split to give t_{2g} and eg subsets and the D ground term states into T2g and Eg, (where upper case is used to denote states and lower case orbitals). f orbitals are split to give subsets known as t_{1g}, t_{2g} and a_{2g}. By analogy, the F ground term when split by a crystal field will give states known as T_{1g}, T_{2g}, and A_{2g}.

Splitting of energy states corresponding to d_n terms

Term	Degeneracy	States in an octahedral field
S	1	A_{1g}
P	3	T_{1g}
D	5	$E_g + T_{2g}$
F	7	$A_{2g} + T_{1g} + T_{2g}$
G	9	$A_{1g} + E_g + T_{1g} + T_{2g}$
H	11	$E_g + T_{1g} + T_{1g} + T_{2g}$
I	13	$A_{1g} + A_{2g} + E_g + T_{1g} + T_{2g} + T_{2g}$

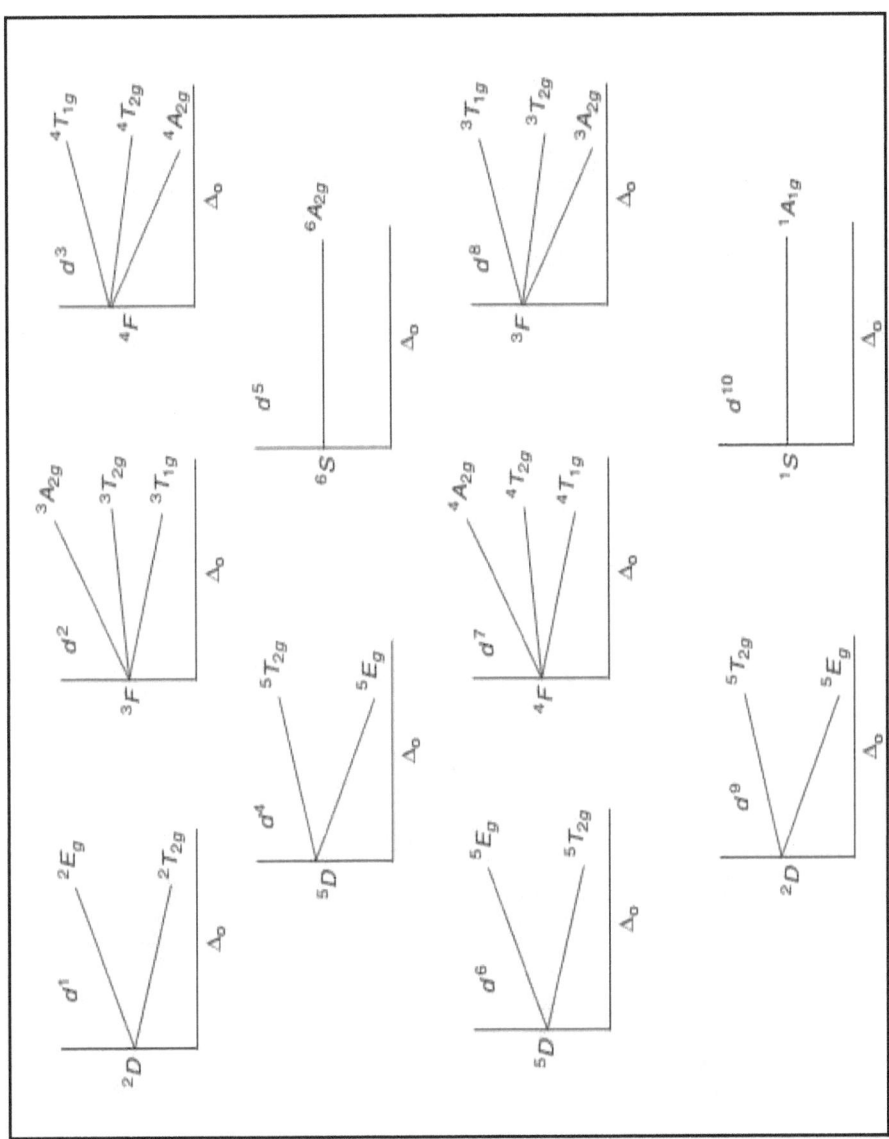

Figure: Splitting patterns for ground-state D and F terms in an octahedral field.

To explain the electronic spectra of complexes generally three types of energy level diagram are used:

(i) Orgel Diagram(ii) Tanabe-Sugano diagram

(iii) Correlation diagram

Orgel Diagram

Orgel diagrams are restricted to only show weak field (i.e. high spin) cases, and offer no information about strong field (low spin) cases. Because Orgel diagrams are qualitative, no energy calculations can be performed from these diagrams; also, this represents the ground and excited states of the same multiplicity for a particular configuration. Excited states of other multiplicities are not considered and hence the diagram is simple. Orgel diagrams will, however, show the number of spin allowed transitions, along with their respective symmetry designations. Terms having different symmetries will cross, while terms having identical symmetries will not cross. In an Orgel diagram, the parent term (P, D, or F) in the presence of no ligand field is located in the center of the diagram, with the terms due to that electronic configuration in a ligand field at each side.

There are two Orgel diagrams, one for d^1, d^4, d^6, and d^9 configurations and the other with d^2, d^3, d^7, and d^8 configurations.

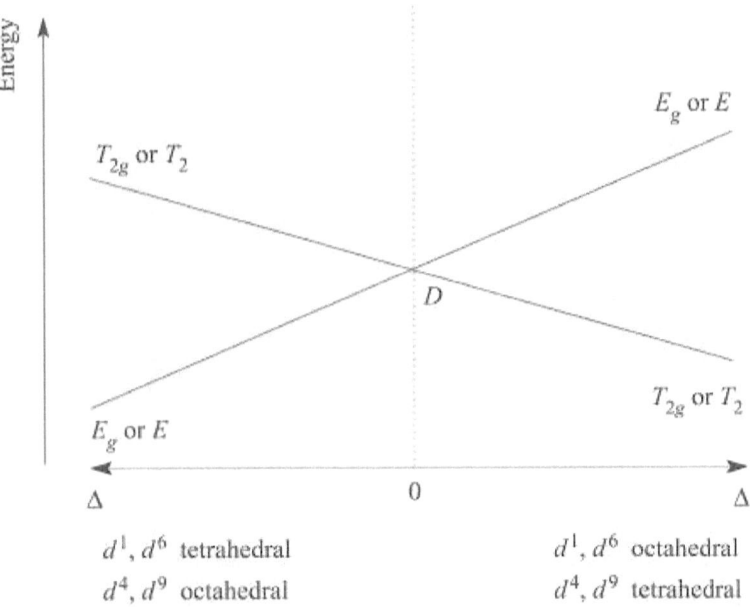

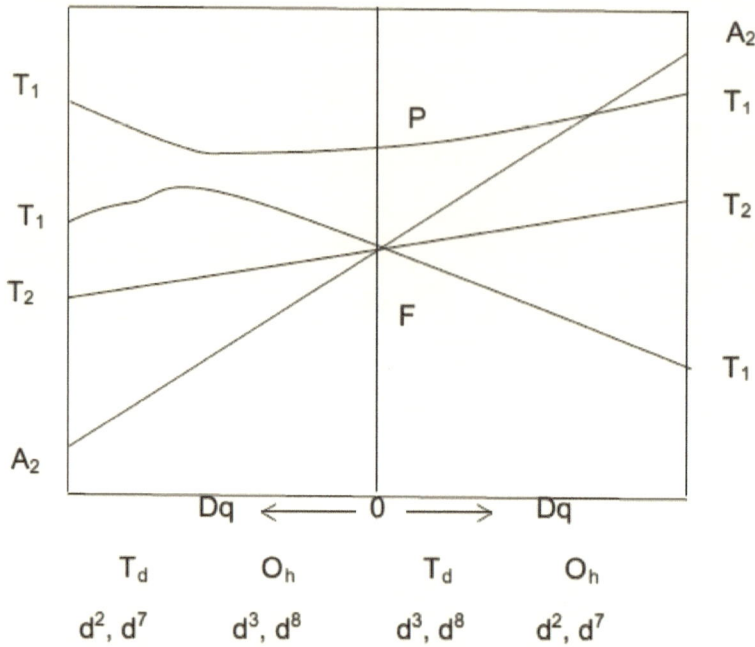

In an Orgel diagram lines with the same Russell – Saunders terms will **diverge due to the non-crossing rule**, but all other lines will be linear. Also, for the D Orgel diagram, the left side contains d^1 and d^6 tetrahedral and d^4 and d^9 octahedral complexes. The right side contains d^4 and d^9 tetrahedral and d^1 and d^6 octahedral complexes. For the F Orgel diagram, the left side contains d^2 and d^7 tetrahedral and d^3 and d^8 octahedral complexes. The right side contains d^3 and d^8 tetrahedral and d^2 and high spin d^7 octahedral complexes.

How to use this diagram?

For example we want to predict the number of transitions for a d2system. Go to the right side of the diagram because Oh-d2 is there. The ground term is T1 arising from the F term of the free ion. Hence, it is denoted as 3T1g(F). Then the probable number of transitions will be: 3T1g(F)3

$$^3T_{1g}(F) \longrightarrow {}^3T_{2g}$$

$$^3T_{1g}(F) \longrightarrow {}^3T_{1g}(P)$$

$$^3T_{1g}(F) \longrightarrow {}^3A_{2g}$$

Order of transitions based on energy

Among the three, the lowest energy transition will be obviously

$$^3T_{1g}(F) \longrightarrow {}^3T_{2g},$$

Which is the next transition amongst the other two depends on the Dqvalue (ligand field strength) as evident from the figure. Till certain point,3A2g has the lower energy than3T1g(P). Hence, in this range of Dq,

$$^3T_{1g}(F) \longrightarrow {}^3A_{2g}$$

will be the second transition. After this point,3T1g (P) term falls in energy and the order is reversed. Hence,

$$^3T1g(F) \longrightarrow {}^3T1g(P)$$

the transitions and their order of energy in the electronic spectrum or when the spectrum is available, it can be interpreted. will be the second transition. Thus, the Orgel diagram of a particular system helps in predicting

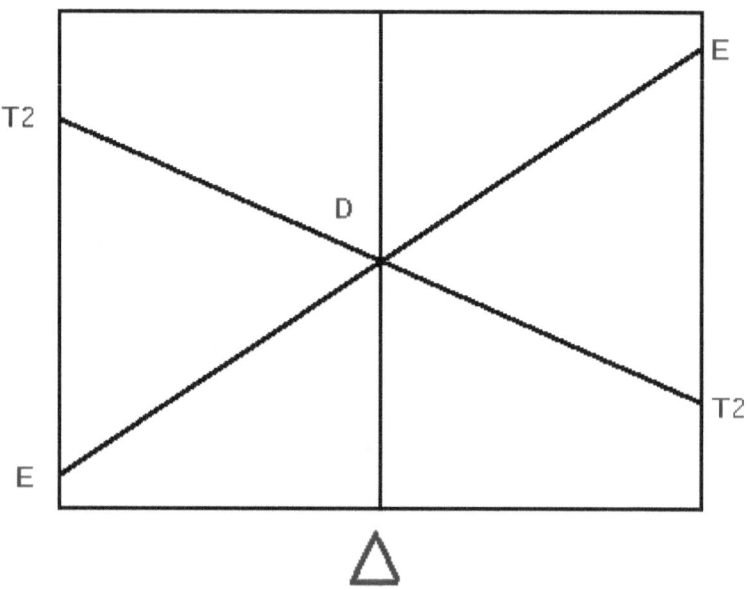

Fig: D- Orgel diagram

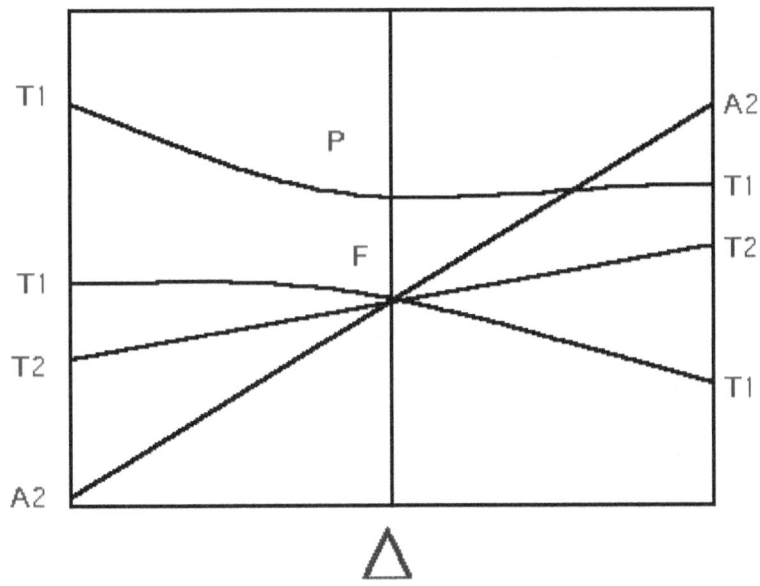

Fig: F& P Orgel diagram

In an Orgel diagram lines with the same Russell – Saunders terms will diverge due to the non-crossing rule, but all other lines will be linear. Also, for the D Orgel diagram, the left side contains d^1 and d^6 tetrahedral and d^4 and d^9 octahedral complexes. The right side contains d^4 and d^9 tetrahedral and d1 and d6 octahedral complexes. For the F Orgel diagram, the left side contains d^2 and d^7 tetrahedral and d^3 and d^8 octahedral complexes. The right side contains d^3 and d^8 tetrahedral and d^2 and high spin d^7 octahedral complex. On the left hand side, the first transition corresponds to D, the equation to calculate the second contains expressions with both D and C.I. (the configuration interaction from repulsion of like terms) and the third has expressions which contain D, C.I. and the Racah parameter B.

1. $^4T_{2g} \longleftarrow {}^4A_{2g}$ transition energy $= D$
2. $^4T_{1g}(F) \longleftarrow {}^4A_{2g}$ transition energy $= 9/5 *D - $ C.I.
3. $^4T_{1g}(P) \longleftarrow {}^4A_{2g}$ transition energy $= 6/5 *D + 15B' + $ C.I.

On the right hand side, the first transition can be unambiguously assigned as:

$^3T_{2g} \longleftarrow {}^3T_{1g}$ transition energy $= 4/5 *D + $ C.I.

But, depending on the size of the ligand field (D) the second transition may be due to:

$^3A_{2g} \longleftarrow {}^3T_{1g}$ transition energy $= 9/5 *D + $ C.I.

for a weak field or

$^3T_{1g}(P) \longleftarrow {}^3T_{1g}$ transition energy $= 3/5 *D + 15B' + 2 * $ C.I.

for a strong field.

Orgel diagram helps in predicting the number of transitions expected in an electronic spectrum (UV-vis) for a complex.

Example 1 $[V(H_2O)_6]^{3+}$

The electronic spectrum of this complex is given in Figure

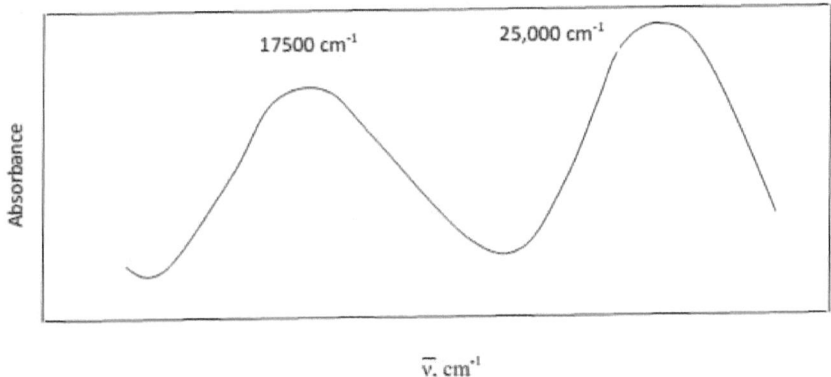

Absorption spectrum of $[V(H_2O)_6]^{3+}$

This spectrum shows two absorption maxima indicating that there are two transitions for this complex and two excited states are there. These two are identified as follows:

Step 1: Find out the oxidation state of the central metal atom in the complex and hence the d^n system

vanadium is in the +3 state in this complex

Electronic configuration of V is: $3d^3 4s^2$

Electronic configuration of $V^{3+}$is: $3d^2$

This complex is an octahedral complex (because six aquo ligands are there) and a d^2 system

Step 2: Find out the ground term of the free ion and how it is split into various energy levels in an octahedral field The ground state for a d^2 system is ^3F. This is split in an octahedral field as shown in Figure

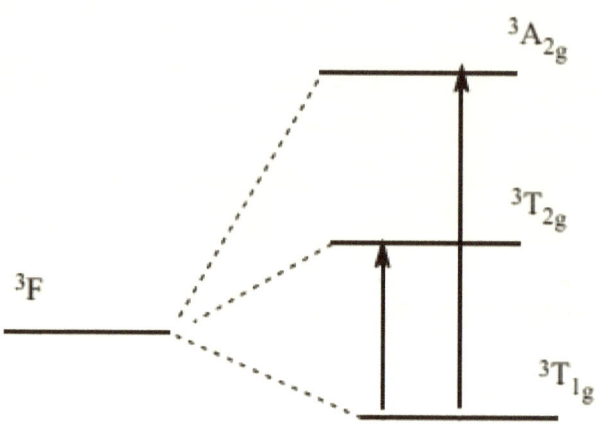

Splitting of an F term in an octahedral field

Step 3: Find out how many excited states with the same multiplicity are thereand hence, how many transitions.

Two excited states with the same multiplicities are there: $^3T_{2g}$ and $^3A_{2g}$.

Therefore, two spin-allowed transitions are possible

$^3T_{ig} \rightarrow {}^3T_{2g}$ will have lower energy and $^3T_{ig} \rightarrow {}^3A_{2g}$ will have lower energy and

Step 4: Based on these can we assign the spectral bands to the transitions?

No, because we have not considered the other terms coming from the excited states and how these are affected by ligand fields. In the excited states, leaving those with multiplicities other than 3, we have got one ^3P state in the free ion, which also transforms as ^3F state in the octahedral field. This is represented as $^3F(P)$. Hence, one more transition is possible for this complex, viz.,

$$^3T_{1g} \longrightarrow {}^3F(P).$$

Step 5: Correct assignment of transitions

This can be done only when we understand the effect of ligand fields on these terms. For example, the $^3F(P)$ will be having higher energy than $3F$ inweak field case, that is, the ligands will be weak ligands. However, when the ligand field strength increases, the energy of $^3F(P)$ decreases and at a particular time, it has a lower energy than $3F$. Under these circumstances, the second transition will be

$$^3T_{1g} \longrightarrow {}^3F(P)$$

and not

$$^3T_{1g} \longrightarrow {}^3F$$

Thus, the variation of energy of terms with respect to ligand field must be known to assign the transitions correctly.

Ground and Excited terms with same multiplicities for weak field Oh and Td complexes		
Configuration	Ground Term (g subscript only for Oh)	Excited terms
d^1(Oh) d^9 (Td)	$^2T_{2g}$	$^2E_{2g}$
d^2(Oh) d^8 (Td)	$^3T_{1g}(F)$	$^3T_{2g}$, $^3A_{2g}$, $^3T_{1g}$ (P)
d^3(Oh) d^7 (Td)	$^4A_{2g}$	$^4T_{2g}$, $^4T_{1g}(F)$, , $^4T_{1g}(P)$,
d^4(Oh) d^6 (Td)	$^5E_{2g}$	$^2T_{2g}$
d^5(Oh) d^5 (Td)	$^6A_{1g}$	-
d^6 (Oh) d^4 (Td)	$^5T_{2g}$	$^5E_{2g}$
d^7 (Oh) d^3 (Td)	$^{43}T_{1g}(F)$	$^4T_{2g}$, $^4A_{2g}$, $^4T_{1g}$ (P)
d^8 (Oh) d^2 (Td)	$^4A_{2g}$	$^3T_{2g}$, $^3T_{1g}(F)$, , $^3T_{1g}(P)$,
d^9 (Oh) d^1 (Td)	$^2E_{2g}$	$^2T_{2g}$

Tanabe-Sugano diagrams

Tanabe–Sugano diagrams can be used for both high spin and low spin complexes, unlike Orgel diagrams, which apply only to high spin complexes. Tanabe–Sugano diagrams can also be used to predict the size of the ligand field necessary to cause high-spin to low-spin transitions. In a Tanabe–Sugano diagram, the ground state is used as a constant reference, in contrast to Orgel diagrams. The energy of the ground state is taken to be zero for all field strengths, and the energies of all other terms and their components are plotted with respect to the ground term.

The x-axis of a Tanabe–Sugano diagram is expressed in terms of the ligand field splitting parameter, Dq, or Δ, divided by the Racah parameter B. The y-axis is in terms of energy, E, also scaled by B. Three Racah parameters exist, A, B, and C, which describe various aspects of interelectronic repulsion. A is an average total interelectron repulsion. B and C correspond with individual d-electron repulsions. A is constant among d-electron configuration, and it is not necessary for calculating relative energies, hence its absence from Tanabe and Sugano's studies of complex ions. C is necessary only in certain cases. B is the most important of Racah's parameters in this case. One line corresponds to each electronic state. The bending of certain lines is due to the mixing of terms with the same symmetry. Although electronic transitions are only "allowed" if the spin multiplicity remains the same (i.e. electrons do not change from spin up to spin down or vice versa when moving from one energy level to another), energy levels for "spin-forbidden" electronic states are included in the diagrams, which are also not included in Orgel diagrams. Each state is given its symmetry label (e.g. A_{1g}, T_{2g}, etc.), but "g" and "u" subscripts are usually left off because it is understood that all the states are gerade. Labels for each state are usually written on the right side of the table, though for more complicated diagrams (e.g. d^6) labels may be written in other locations for clarity. Term symbols (e.g. ^3P, ^1S, etc.) for a specific dn free ion are listed, in order of increasing energy, on the y-axis of the diagram. The relative order of energies is determined using Hund's rules.

This diagram results when the energy of various terms are plotted against B, where B is the Racah parameter (interelectronic repulsion parameter). Tanabe Sugano diagrams, which are able to predict the transition energies for both spin-allowed and spin-forbidden transitions, as well as for both strong field (low spin), and weak field (high spin) complexes. This diagram hence more useful and understandable than Orgel diagrams.

Quantitative information can be obtained from this diagram. Weak field complexes are left of the vertical line in the middle and the strong field cases are on the right of the vertical line in the middle. In this method the energy of the electronic states are given on the vertical axis and the ligand field strength increases on the horizontal axis from left to right. Linear lines are found when there are no other terms of the same type and curved lines are found when two or more terms are repeated. This is as a result of the "non-crossing rule". The baseline in the Tanabe-Sugano diagram represents the lowest energy or ground term state.

Advantages over Orgel diagrams

In Orgel diagrams, the magnitude of the splitting energy exerted by the ligands on d orbitals, as a free ion approach a ligand field, is compared to the electron-repulsion energy, which are both sufficient at providing the placement of electrons. However, if the ligand field splitting energy, 10Dq, is greater than the electron-repulsion energy, then Orgel diagrams fail in determining electron placement. In this case, Orgel diagrams are restricted to only high spin complexes.

Tanabe–Sugano diagrams do not have this restriction, and can be applied to situations when 10Dq is significantly greater than electron repulsion. Thus, Tanabe–Sugano diagrams are utilized in determining electron placements for high spin and low spin metal complexes. However, they are limited in that they have only qualitative significance. Even so, Tanabe–Sugano diagrams are useful in interpreting UV-vis spectra and determining the value of 10Dq.

TS Diagram for d^n

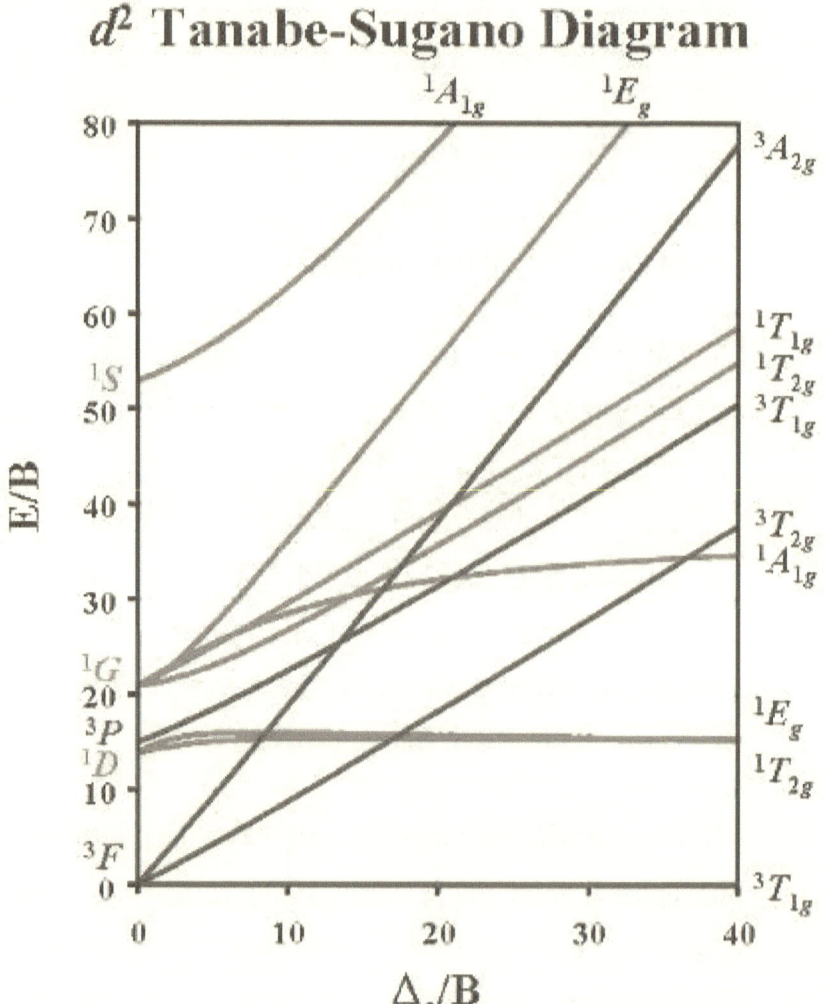

d^2 **Tanabe-Sugano Diagram**

d^3 Tanabe-Sugano Diagram

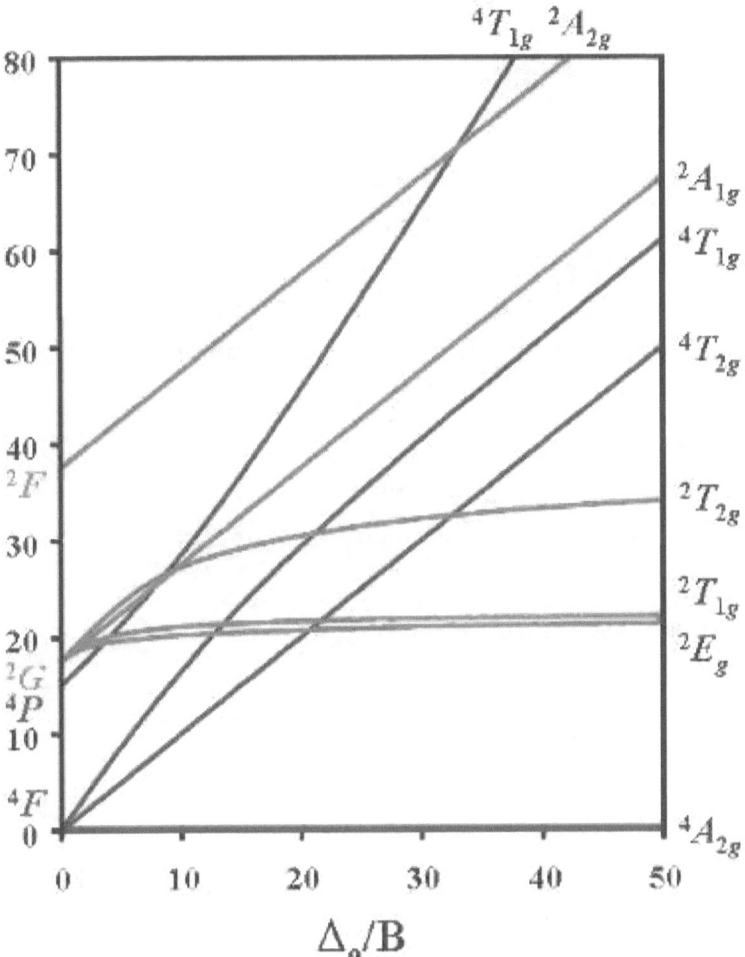

d^4 Tanabe-Sugano Diagram

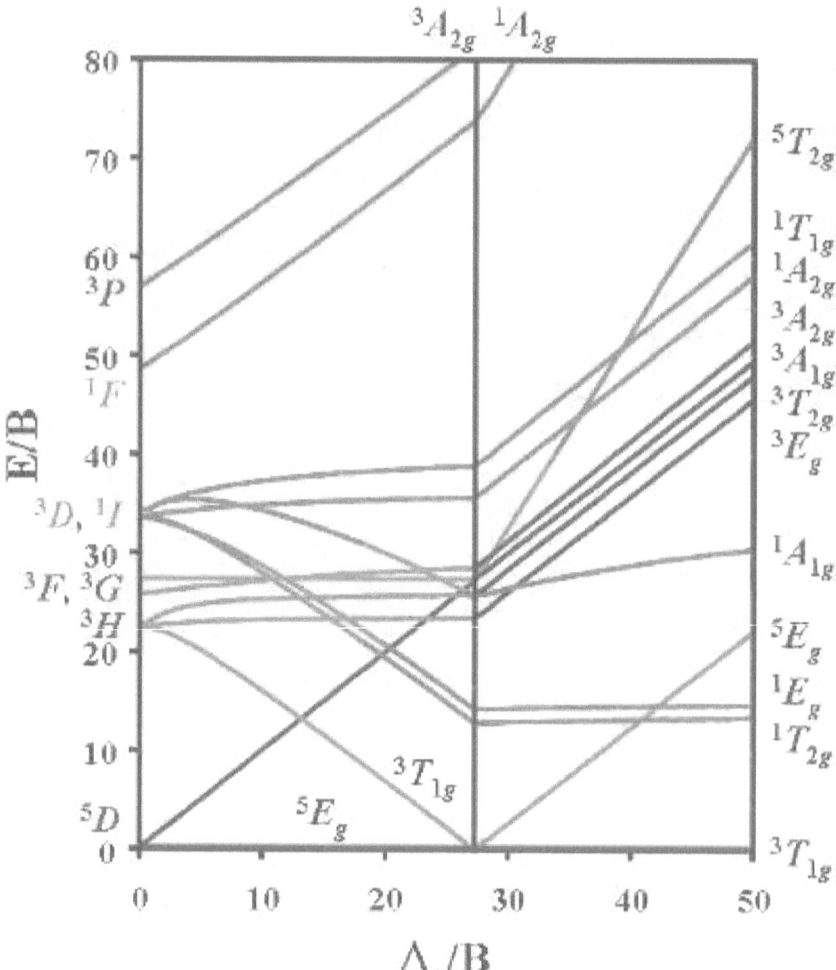

d^5 Tanabe-Sugano Diagram

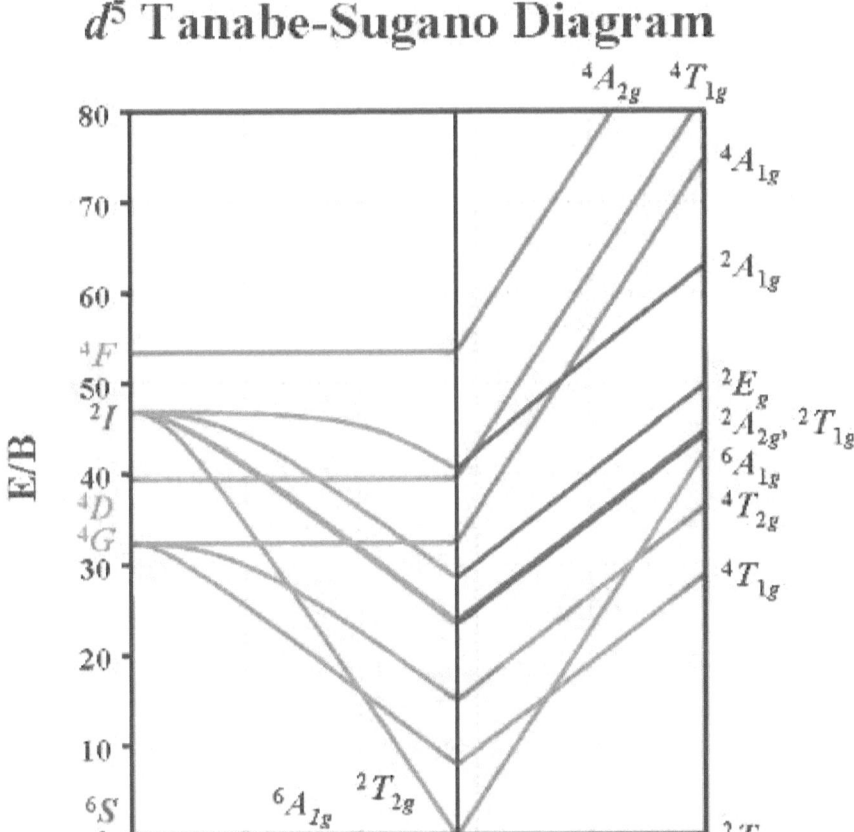

d^6 Tanabe-Sugano Diagram

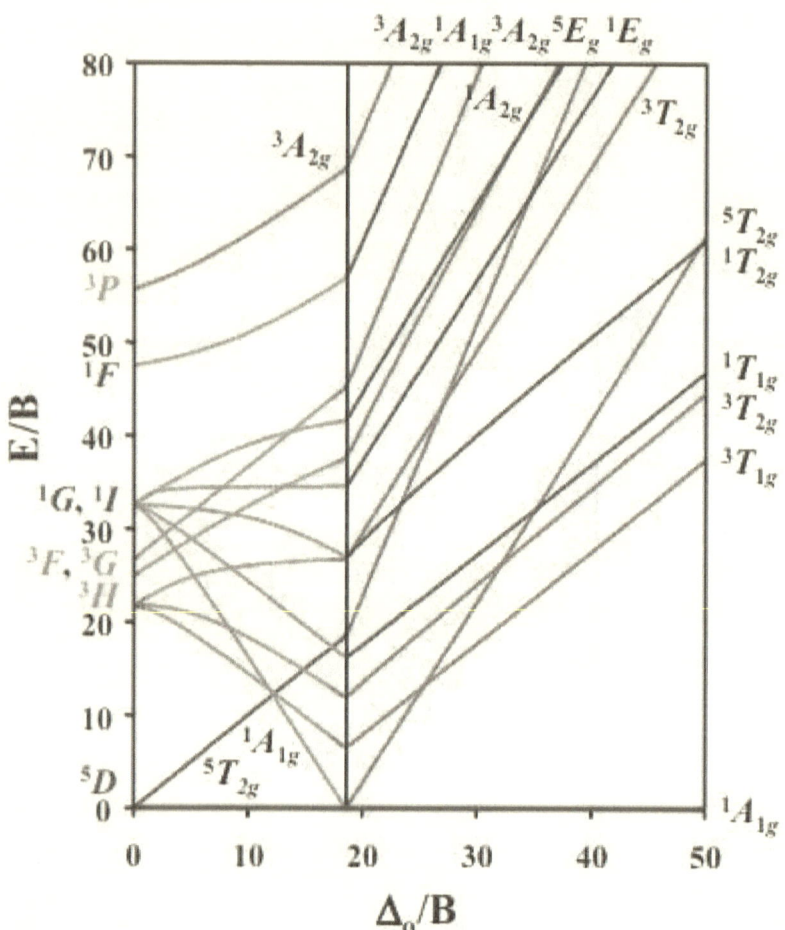

d^7 Tanabe-Sugano Diagram

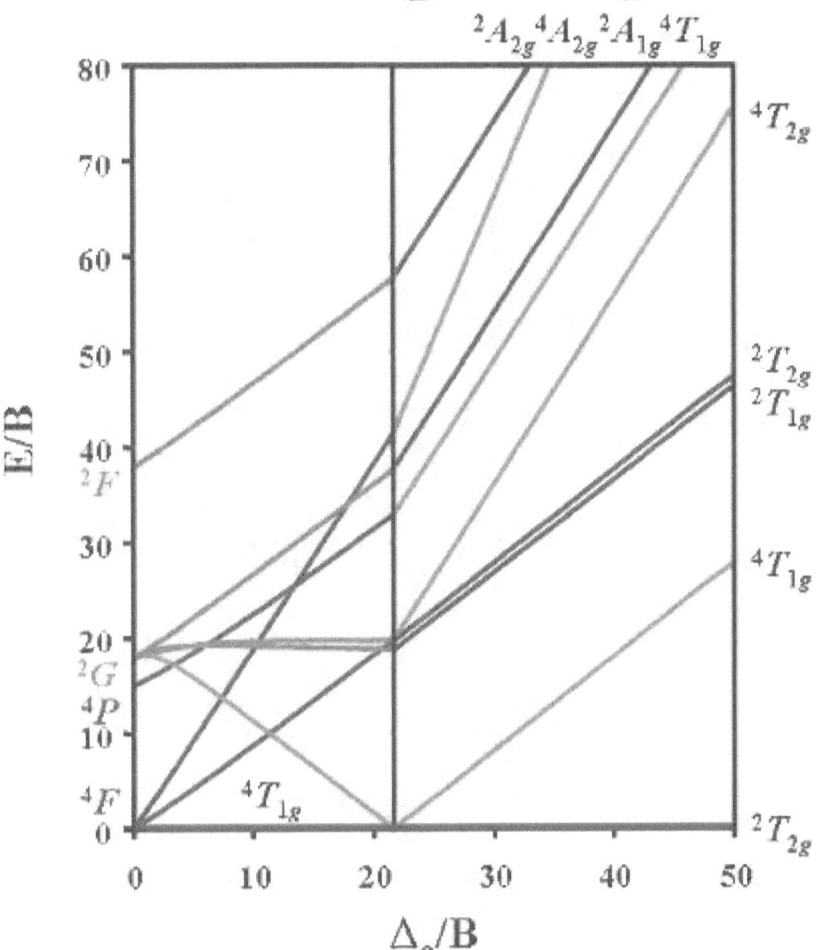

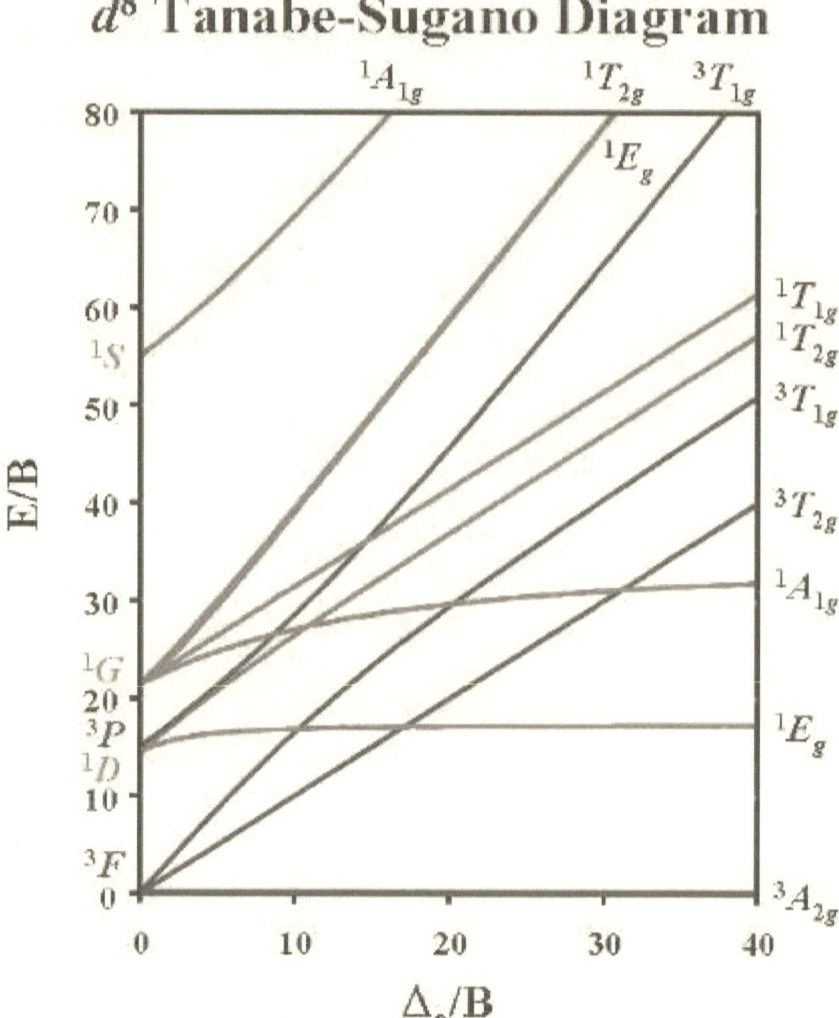

d^8 Tanabe-Sugano Diagram

Unnecessary diagrams: d^1, d^9 and d^{10}

There is no electron repulsion in a d^1 complex, and the single electron resides in the t_{2g} orbital ground state. A d^1 octahedral metal complex, such as $[Ti(H_2O)_6]^{3+}$, shows a single absorption band in a UV-vis experiment. The term symbol for d^1 is ^2D, which splits into the $^2T_{2g}$ and ^2E_g states. The t_{2g} orbital set holds the single electron and has a $^2T_{2g}$ state energy of -4Dq. When that electron is promoted to an e_g orbital, it is excited to the ^2E_g state energy, +6Dq. This is in accordance with the single absorption band in a UV-vis experiment. The prominent shoulder in this absorption band is due to a Jahn-Teller distortion which removes the degeneracy of the two ^2E_g states. However, since these two transitions overlap in a UV-vis spectrum, this transition from $^2T_{2g}$ to ^2E_g does not require a Tanabe–Sugano diagram.

d^9

Similar to d^1 metal complexes, d^9 octahedral metal complexes have ^2D spectral term. The transition is from the $(t_{2g})^6(e_g)^3$ configuration (^2E_g state) to the $(t_{2g})^5(eg)^4$ configuration (2T2g state). This could also be described as a positive "hole" that moves from the e_g to the t_{2g} orbital set. The sign of Dq is opposite that for d^1, with a ^2E_g ground state and a $^2T_{2g}$ excited state. Like the d^1 case, d^9 octahedral complexes do not require the Tanabe–Sugano diagram to predict their absorption spectra.

d^{10}

There are no d-d electron transitions in d^{10} metal complexes because the d orbitals are completely filled. Thus, UV-vis absorption bands are not observed and a Tanabe–Sugano diagram does not exist.

Example 1: The d^2 case

The electronic spectrum of the V^{3+} ion, where V(III) is doped into alumina (Al_2O_3), shows three major peaks with frequencies of: $n_1 = 17400$ cm^{-1}, $n_2 = 25400$ cm^{-1} and $n_3 = 34500$ cm^{-1}.

These have been assigned to the following spin-allowed transitions.

3T2g   ←   3T1g

3T1g(P) ←   3T1g

3A2g   ←   3T1g

The ratio between the first two transitions is calculated as n_2 / n_1 which is equal to $25400 / 17400 = 1.448$.

In order to calculate the Racah parameter, B, the position on the horizontal axis where the ratio between the lines representing n2 and n1 is equal to 1.448, has to be determined. On the diagram below, this occurs at D/B=30.9. Having found this value, a vertical line is drawn at this position.

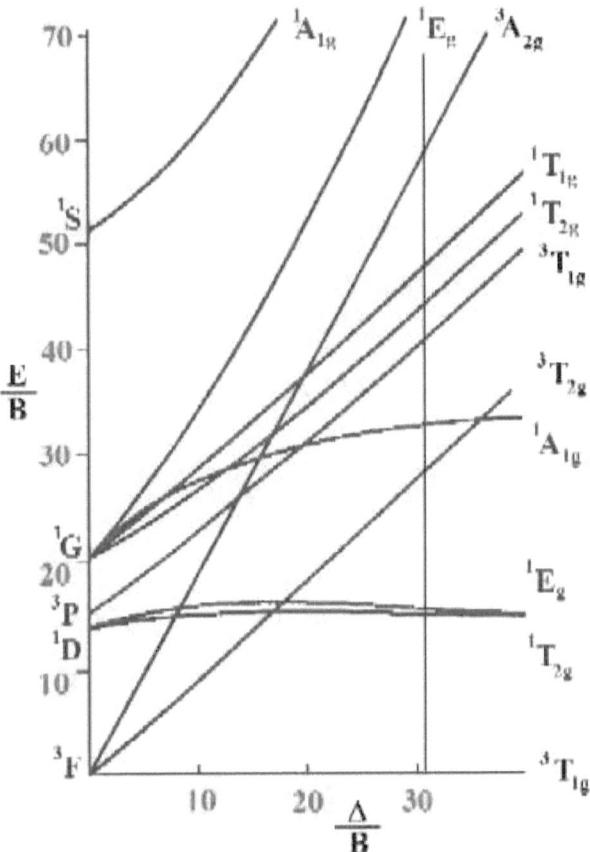

On moving up the line from the ground term to where lines from the other terms cross it, we are able to identify both the spin-forbidden and spin-allowed transition and hence the total number of transitions that are possible in the electronic spectrum.

Next, find the values on the vertical axis that correspond to the spin-allowed transitions so as to determine the values of n1/B, n2/B and n3/B. From the diagram above these are 28.78, 41.67 and 59.68 respectively.

Knowing the values of n1, n2 and n3, we can now calculate the value of B.

Since n1/B=28.78 and n1 is equal to 17,400 cm^{-1}, then

B=n1/28.78 = 17400/28.78 or B=604.5cm^{-1}

Then it is possible to calculate the value of D. Since D/B=30.9, then: D=B*30.9 and hence: D = 604.5 * 30.9 = 18680 cm^{-1}

Example 1: The d^3 case

Calculate the value of B and D for the Cr^{3+} ion in $[Cr(H_2O)_6)]^{3+}$ if n1=17000 cm^{-1}, n2=24000 cm^{-1} and n3=37000 cm^{-1}.

SOLUTION

These values have been assigned to the following spin-allowed transitions.

$^4T_{2g}$ <--- $^4A_{2g}$

$^4T_{1g}$ <--- $^4A_{2g}$

$^4T_{1g}(P)$ <--- $^4A_{2g}$

From the information given, the ratio

$n2 / n1 =$

$24000 / 17000 = 1.412$

Using a Tanabe-Sugano diagram for a d3 system this ratio is found at $D/B=24.00$

Tanabe-Sugano diagram for d3 octahedral complexes

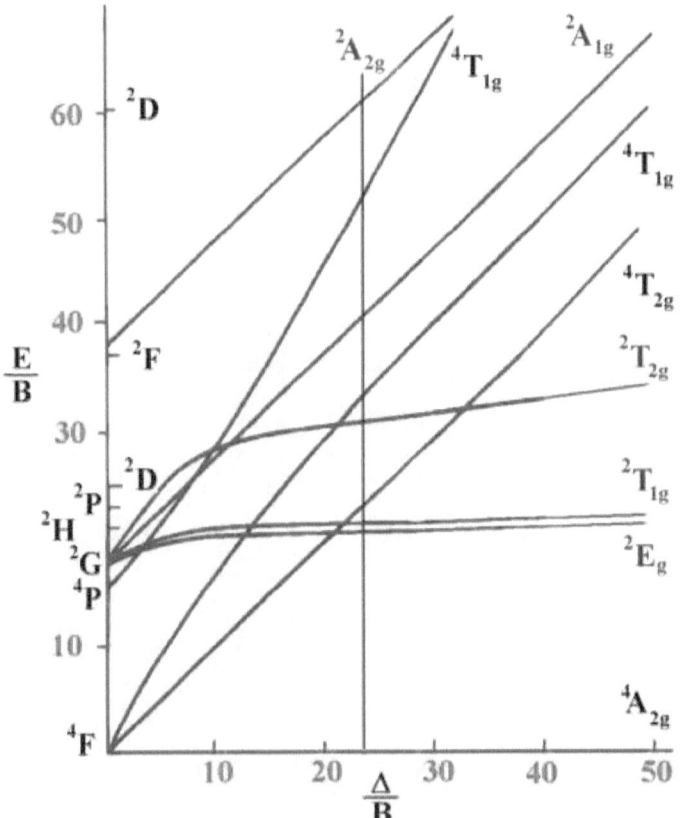

Interpolation of the graph to find the Y-axis values for the spin-allowed transitions gives:

- $n1/B = 24.00$
- $n2/B = 33.90$
- $n3/B = 53.11$

Recall that $n1 = 17000$ cm^{-1}. Therefore for the first spin-allowed transition, $17000 / B = 24.00$ from which B can be obtained, $B = 17000 / 24.00$ or $B = 708.3$ cm^{-1}.

This information is then used to calculate D.

Since $D / B = 24.00$ then $D = B * 24.00 = 708.3 * 24.00$

$= 17000$ cm^{-1}.

It is observed that the value of **Racah parameter** B in the complex is 708.3 cm^{-1}, while the value of B in the free Cr^{3+} ion is 1030 cm^{-1}. This shows a 31% reduction in the Racah parameter indicating a strong Nephelauxetic effect.

The Nephelauxetic Series is as follows:

$F^- > H_2O > urea > NH_3 > en \sim C_2O_4^{2-} > NCS^- > Cl^- \sim CN^- > Br^- > S^{2-} \sim I^-$.

Ionic ligands such as F$^-$ give small reduction in B, while covalently bonded ligands such as I⁻ give a large reduction in B.

The diagram is for a d6 system. is shown in Figure. From this diagram, weak and strong field spectra can be assigned for Co (III) complexes. Thus, for CoF63-, there will be only one transition, viz

$$^5T_{2g} \longrightarrow \quad ^5E_g$$

and in the case of Co(NH3)63+, there will be a minimum of two transitions, viz.

$$^1A_{1g} \rightarrow {}^1T_{1g}$$

and

$$^1A_{1g} \rightarrow {}^1T_{2g}$$

These are shown by vertical arrows in the diagram. These are the spin-allowed transitions.

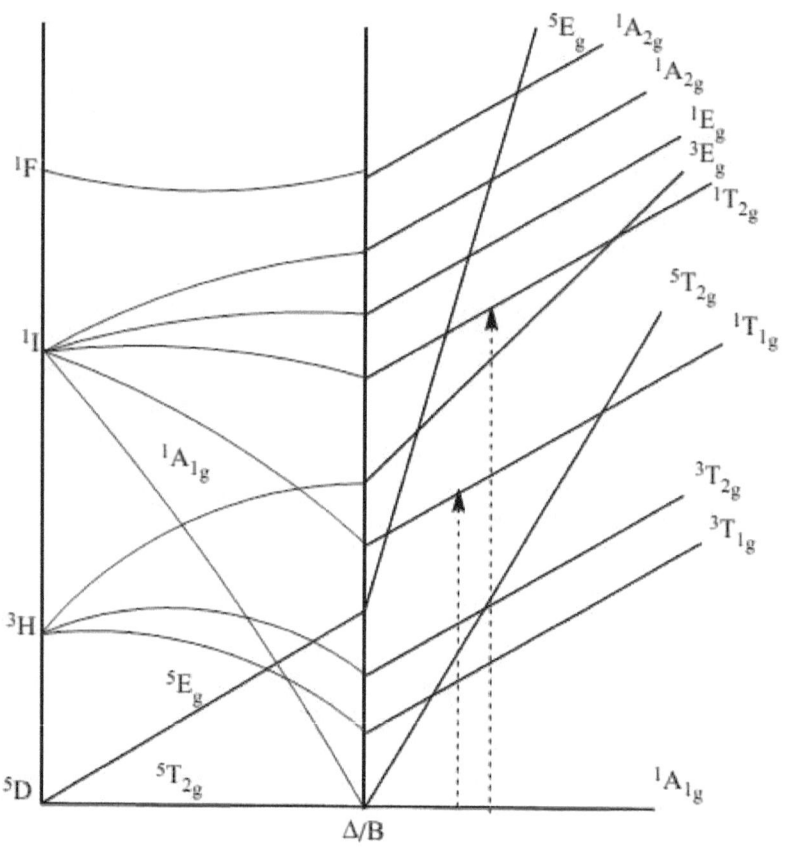

Tanabe-Sugano diagram for d6 octahedral complex

Manganese(II) hexahydrate

In the $[Mn(H_2O)_6]^{2+}$ metal complex, manganese has an oxidation state of +2, thus it is a d^5 ion. H_2O is a weak field ligand (spectrum shown below), and according to the Tanabe–Sugano diagram for d^5 ions, the ground state is $^6A_1$. Note that there is no sextet spin multiplicity in any excited state, hence the transitions from this ground state are expected to be spin-forbidden and the band intensities should be low. From the spectra, only very low intensity bands are observed (low Molar absorptivity (ε) values on y-axis).

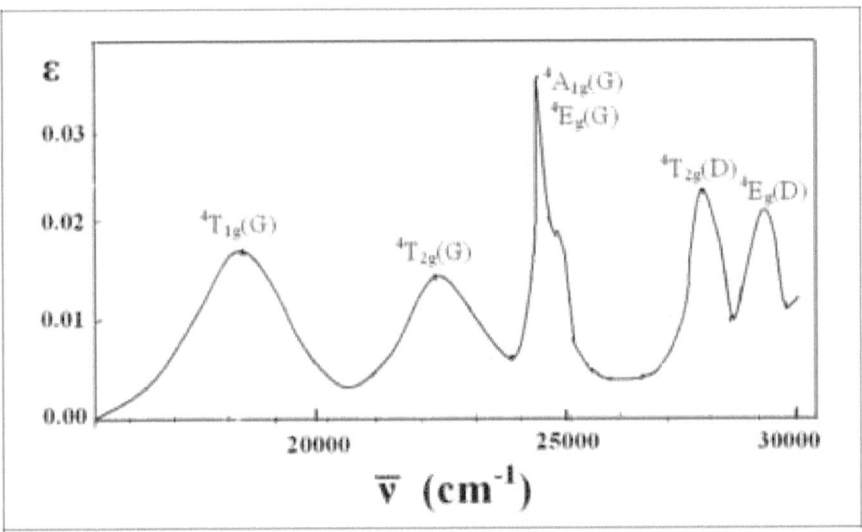

Cobalt(II) hexahydrate

Another example is $[Co(H_2O)_6]^{2+}$ Note that the ligand is the same as the last example. Here the cobalt ion has the oxidation state of +2, and it is a d^7 ion. From the high-spin (left) side of the d^7 Tanabe–Sugano diagram, the ground state is $^4T_1(F)$, and the spin multiplicity is a quartet. The diagram shows that there are three quartet excited states: $^4T_2$, $^4A_2$, and $^4T_1(P)$. From the diagram one can predict that there are three spin-allowed transitions. However, the spectra of $[Co(H_2O)_6]^{2+}$ does not show three distinct peaks that correspond to the three predicted excited states. Instead, the spectrum has a broad peak (spectrum shown below). Based on the T-S diagram, the lowest energy transition is $^4T_1$ to $^4T_2$, which is seen in the near IR and is not observed in the visible spectrum. The main peak is the energy transition $^4T_1(F)$ to $^4T_1(P)$, and the slightly higher energy transition (the shoulder) is predicted to be $^4T_1$ to $^4A_2$. The small energy difference leads to the overlap of the two peaks, which explains the broad peak observed in the visible spectrum.

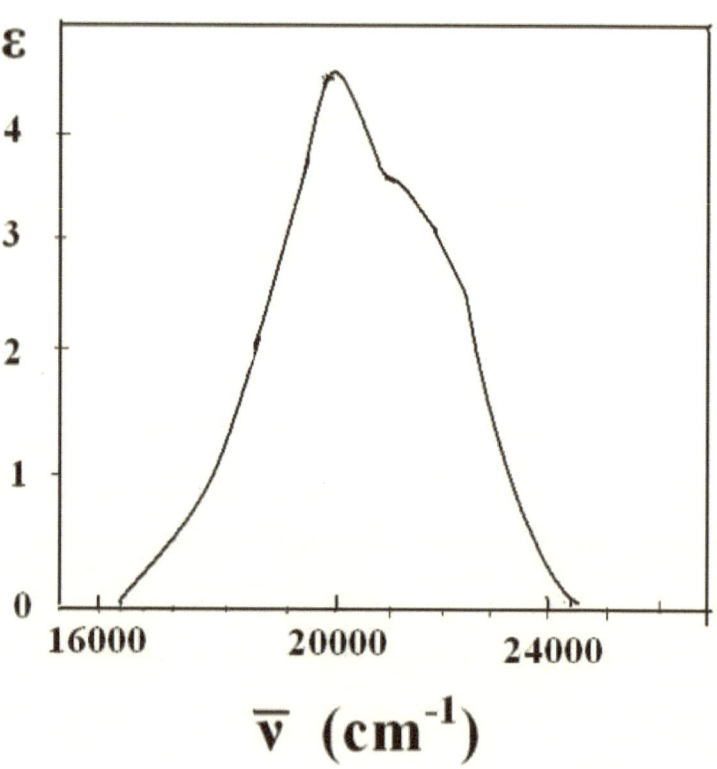

Tetrahedral Complexes

The same octahedral Tanabe - Sugano diagrams can be used for tetrahedral complexes. However, for a dn tetrahedral complex, the d(10-n)Tanabe-Sugano diagram must be used (i.e. for d8Td, use the d2O hT-S diagram)

Some important general observations from the Tanabe - Sugano diagrams are:

(i) Some lines are curved. This arises because whenever two states of the same symmetry (same term symbol) are close in energy, they can be combined to yield one state of lower energy and another of higher energy. In a Tanabe-Sugano diagram, this makes it appear that some lines bend away from each other to avoid crossing. As a result, this phenomenon is referred to as the "noncrossing rule". Note that transitions involving these curved lines must be avoided when determining Dq from Tanabe - Sugano diagrams

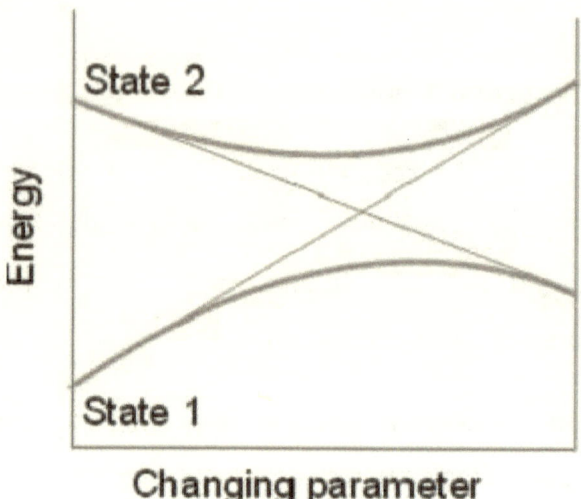

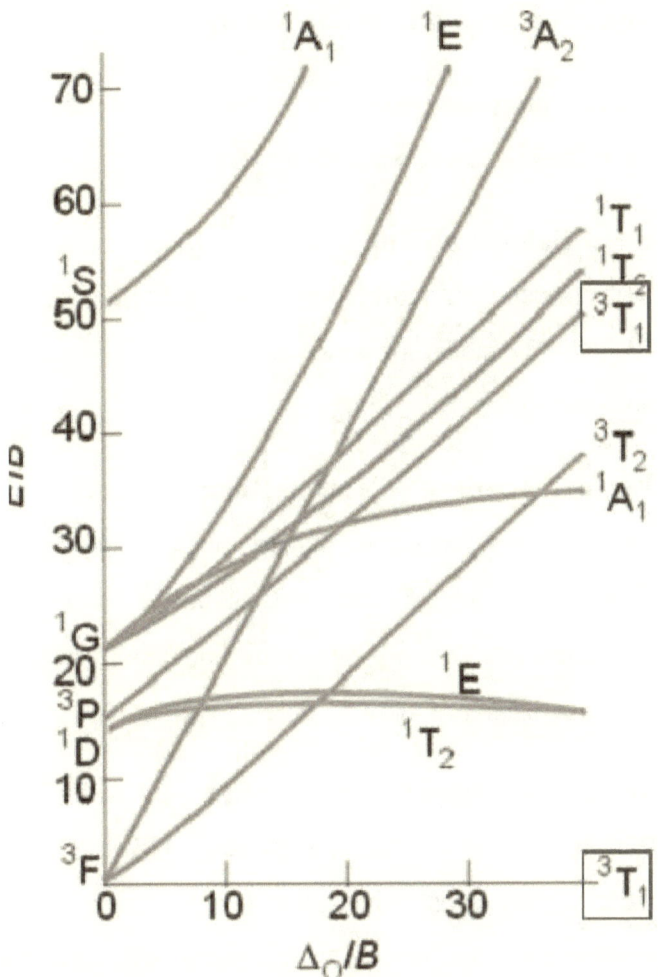

(ii)   For some configurations, there is an abrupt change of slope and the ground state term also changes. This happens when there is a transition from a High- Spin to a Low - Spin state.

Selection rules and molar absorptivity

There are two selection rules which govern the relative intensities of electronic absorption bands:

Spin Selection Rule —Transitions between different spin multiplicities are forbidden. For example, transitions between $^4A_2$ and $^4T_1$ states are spin- allowed, but between $^4A_2$ and $^2A_2$ are spin-forbidden.

Laporte (Parity) Selection Rule —Transitions between states of the same parity (symmetry with respect to inversion) are forbidden. For example, transitions between d - orbitals are forbidden (these are g →g transitions) but transitions between d and p orbitals are allowed (g → u).

These rules would seem to rule out many of the electronic transitions for metal complexes. However, many transition metal complexes are famous for their bright colours; a consequence of various mechanisms by which the above rules can be relaxed. The most important relaxation mechanisms are:

Vibronic Coupling (molecular vibrations) temporarily changes molecular symmetry, and can result in temporary loss of the centre of symmetry in an octahedral complex. This provides a way to relax the Laporte selection rule . As a consequence, d - d transitions often have extinction coefficients (e) of 10 to 100

$dm^3 mol^{-1} cm^{-1}$ which is responsible for the bright colours of many transition metal complexes.

Tetrahedral Complexes absorb more strongly than octahedral complexes. Metal -ligand s- bonding in transition metal complexes of Td symmetry, and the lack of a centre of symmetry makes transitions between d - orbitals more allowed (relaxation of the Laporte selection rule). As a result, extinction coefficients of around $e = 500$ $dm^3 mol^{-1} cm^{-1}$ are common. As a qualitative example, $[Ni(H_2O)_6]^{2+}$ is pale green while $[Ni(PPh_3)_4]^{2+}$ is deep blue

Spin-Orbit Coupling can provide a mechanism for relaxation of the spin selection rule. Such absorption bands for first-row transition metal complexes are generally weak, with typical extinction coefficients of around $e = 1$ $dm^3 mol^{-1} cm^{-1}$.

For example, octahedral Mn^{2+} complexes (d^5) cannot undergo any spin-allowed transitions from the $^6A_1$ ground state, so are extremely pale coloured. By contrast, Spin- Orbit coupling can be more important for 2nd and 3rd row transition metal complexes

The molar absorptivity (e, extinction coefficient) is a good indicator of the type of electronic transition:

Types of transition	ϵ $(dm^3 mol^{-1} cm^{-1})$	Example
Spin forbidden	< 1	$Mn^{2+}(aq)$
d-d laporte forbidden	10-100	Most 3d O_h complexes
d-d non-centrosymmetric system	~500	T_d complexes
π^* -π transition, symmetric allowed	~10,000	Organic chormophors

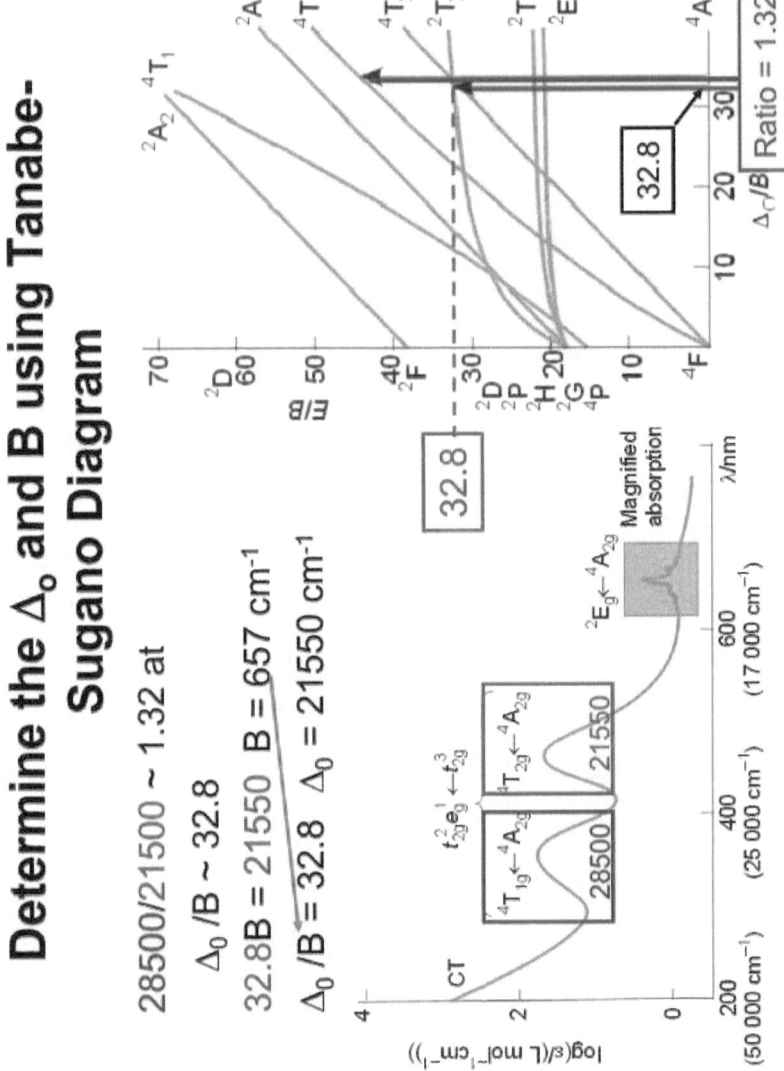

Determine the Δ_o and B using Tanabe-Sugano Diagram

$28500/21500 \sim 1.32$ at

$\Delta_o /B \sim 32.8$

$32.8B = 21550 \quad B = 657 \text{ cm}^{-1}$

$\Delta_o /B = 32.8 \quad \Delta_o = 21550 \text{ cm}^{-1}$

(ii) Correlation Diagram

The LEVER Method

A method described by A. B. P. Lever (1968) provides an extremely simple and rapid means of evaluating Dq and B for metal complexes. In this method, the equations for E (v1), E (v2), and E (v3) are used with a wide range of Dq/ B values to calculate the ratios v3/ v1, v3/ v2, and v2/ v1.

When using the Lever method, experimental band maxima are used to calculate the ratios v3/ v1, v3/ v2, and v2/ v1. The ratios are then located on the appropriate line on the graph, and by reading downward to the horizontal axis, the value of Dq/ B is determined. Once the vi/vj ratio is located, the v3/ B value can also be identified by reading to the right-hand axis, whether or not v3is available from the spectrum. Therefore, because Dq/ B and v3are both known, it is a simple matter to calculate Dq and B. When using the Lever method, it is best to use either the original tables of values or a large-scale graph with grid lines to be able to read values more accurately.

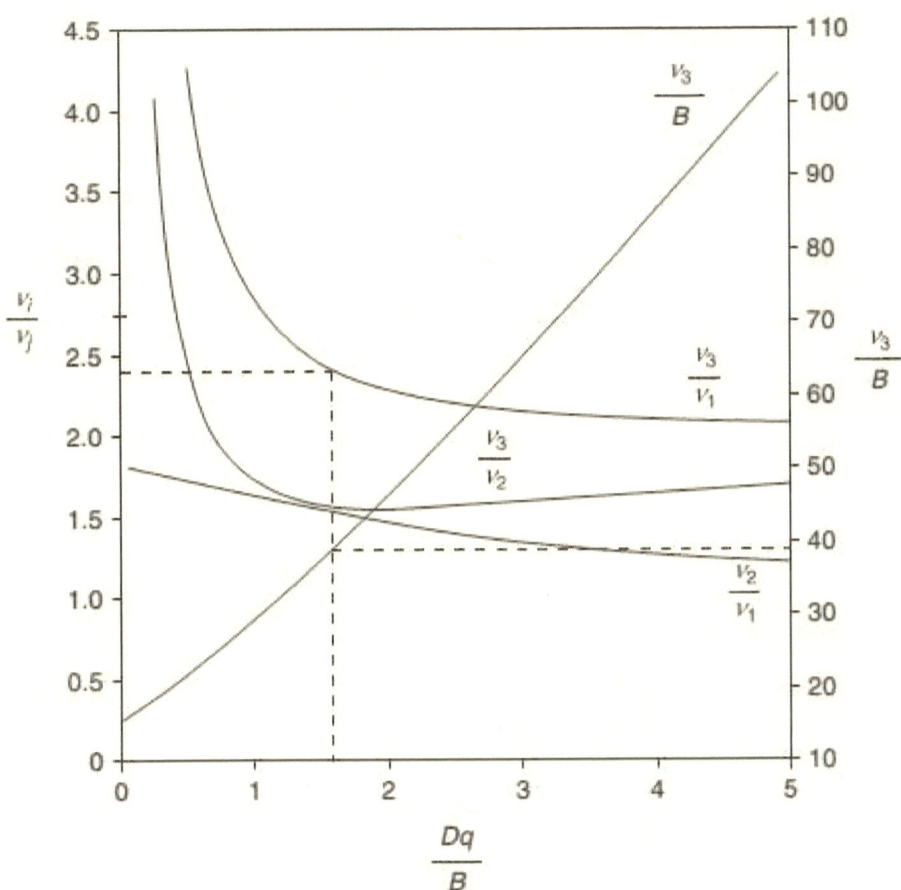

Figure 2: Diagram for using the Lever method to determine Dq and Bfor ions having Aspectroscopic ground states

The procedure for using the Lever method will be illustrated by considering the CrX_6^{3-} complex

described earlier in using the Tanabe-Sugano diagram. In this case, absorption bands were presumed to be seen at 11,000 and 26,500 cm^{-1} and to represent $v1$ and $v3$, respectively. Therefore $v3/v1 = 2.41$. Because Cr^{3+} is a d^3 ion, the ground state is $^4A_{2g}$, so Figure is the appropriate one to use. Reading across to the vertical axis opposite the value $v3/v1 = 2.41$ corresponds to a value of Dq/B equal to about 1.6 on the horizontal axis. Similarly, the value $v3/B$ are found to be about 38.5. Therefore

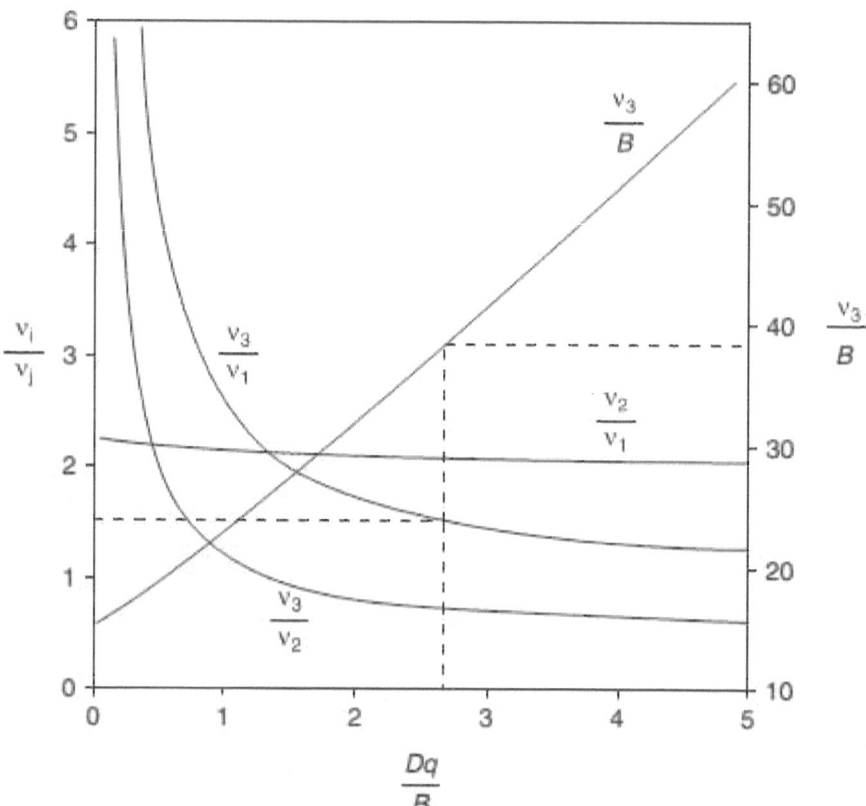

$$Dq/B = 1.6$$

$$\nu_3 / B = 38.5$$

so that $B = Dq/1.6$ and $B = \nu_3/38.5$

Dq = v3 x 1.6/3.85 = 26,500 cm^{-1} x 1.6/.85 =1100 cm^{-1}

which leads to a value of approximately 690 cm^{-1} for B . These values are in fair agreement with the values of 1200 cm^{-1} and 760 cm^{-1} estimated for Dq and B , respectively, from the Tanabe-Sugano diagram. Because B for the gaseous Cr^{3+} ion is 1030 cm^{-1}, the nephelauxetic ratio for this complex is B 690 cm^{-1}/1030 cm^{-1} = 0.67, which is a typical value for this parameter.

When using the Lever method, the question naturally arises regarding the situation in which the identities of the bands in the spectrum are unknown. Assuming that we do not know that the observed bands are actually v1 and v3, we calculate from the previous example that vi/vj = 2.41. It is readily apparent that this ratio could not be v2/v1 because the entire range of values presented for this ratio is approximately 1.2 to 1.8. If the 2.41 value actually represented v3/v2, a value of Dq/ B of about 0.52 is indicated. From our previous discussions, it has been seen that for first-row □ 3 metal ions, Δ o is about 15,000 to 24,000 cm - 1 (Dq approximately 1500 – 2400 cm^{-1}) depending on the ligands. It has also been shown that B values for first-row metals are typically about 800 to 1000 cm^{-1}. Therefore, for this situation a ratio of Dq/ B of 0.52 is clearly out of the realm of possibility for an octahedral complex of this type. For that reason, a ratio of band energies of 2.41 is consistent only with the bands being assigned as v3and v1. It can be shown that this is the case for other complexes as well. It is not actually necessary to know the assignments of the bands in most cases to use the Lever method to determine Dq and B . Assuming that the complexes have realistic values for Dq and B leads to the conclusion that only one set of assignments is possible. Also, only two band positions need to be known because the ratio of these gives the Dq/ B and v3/ B values from the figures.

In the case of VF_6^{3+}, which has bands at 14,800 cm^{-1} and 23,000 cm^{-1}. Because V^{3+} is a d^2 ion, the ground-state term is $^3T_{1g}$, and in this case, v3/ v1= 1.55. From it can be seen (from the dotted lines) that a value of 1.55 for the ratio v3/ v1corresponds to Dq/ B =2.6 and v3/ B = 38. Therefore, using these values it is found that

B= v3/.38   = Dq/ 2 6

so that Dq = 23,000 cm^{-1}1x 2.6/38 = 1600 cm^{-1} and B is 600 cm^{-1}.

These values for Dq and B are in agreement with those obtained for this complex using other procedures. We know that a value of 16,000 cm^{-1} for Δ o is typical of most complexes of a +3 first-row transition metal ion. For V^{3+}, the free-ion B value is 860 cm^{-1}, so the value 600 cm^{-1} found for V^{3+} in the complex indicates a value of 0.70 for the nephelauxetic ratio, β .

All of these values are typical of complexes of first-row transition metal ions. Therefore, even though the identity of the bands may be uncertain, performing the analysis will lead to B and Dq values that will be reasonable only when the correct assignment of the bands has been made.

JØRGENSEN'S METHOD

An interesting approach to predicting the ligand field splitting for a given metal ion and ligand has been given by Christian Klixbüll Jørgensen. In Jørgensen's approach, the equation that has been developed to predict the ligand field splitting in an octahedral field, Δo , is

$$\Delta o (cm^{-1}) = f\, g \dots \dots \dots \dots \dots \dots \dots (1)$$

where f is a parameter characteristic of the ligand and g is a parameter characteristic of the metal ion. The values for parameters in this equation are based on the assignment of a value of $f = 1.00$ for water as a ligand and values for other ligands were determined by fitting the spectral data to known ligand field splitting. Table 1 shows representative values for f and g parameters for several metal ions and ligands.

Eqn (1) predicts values for Δ_o that are in reasonably good agreement with the values determined by more robust methods. In many instances, an approximate value for the ligand field splitting is all that is required, and this approach gives a useful approximation for Δ_o rapidly with a minimum of effort.

Selected Values for the f and g Parameters for use in Jorgensen's Equation			
Metal Ion	**g**	**Ligand**	**f**
Mn^{2+}	8000	Br^-	0.72
Ni^{2+}	8700	SCN^-	0.7
Co^{2+}	9000	Cl^-	0.78
V^{2+}	12000	N_3^-	0.83
Fe^{3+}	14000	F^-	0.90
Cr^{3+}	174000	H_2O	1.00
Co^{3+}	18200	NCS^-	1.02
Ru^{2+}	20000	py	1.23
Rh^{3+}	27000	NH_3	1.25

www.ingramcontent.com/pod-product-compliance
Lightning Source LLC
Chambersburg PA
CBHW020336290526
45785CB00005B/2038